2 ✓ W9-BHZ-697

Read 33 – 45 ①
5 – 16 ②

Read 4th & 6th
Chapters.

LANGUAGE, TRUTH AND LOGIC

by

ALFRED JULES AYER

Grote Professor of the Philosophy of
Mind and Logic at University College, London

DOVER PUBLICATIONS, INC.
NEW YORK

To R. A.

This Dover edition, first published in 1952, is an unabridged and unaltered republication of the second (1946) edition. It is reprinted by special arrangement with Victor Gollantz, Ltd., and is for sale in the United States of America and Canada only.

Standard Book Number: 486-20010-8
Library of Congress Catalog Card Number: 52-860

Manufactured in the United States of America
Dover Publications, Inc.
180 Varick Street
New York, N. Y. 10014

INTRODUCTION

In the ten years that have passed since *Language, Truth and Logic* was first published, I have come to see that the questions with which it deals are not in all respects so simple as it makes them appear; but I still believe that the point of view which it expresses is substantially correct. Being in every sense a young man's book, it was written with more passion than most philosophers allow themselves to show, at any rate in their published work, and while this probably helped to secure it a larger audience than it might have had otherwise, I think now that much of its argument would have been more persuasive if it had not been presented in so harsh a form. It would, however, be very difficult for me to alter the tone of the book without extensively re-writing it, and the fact that, for reasons not wholly dependent upon its merits, it has achieved something of the status of a text-book is, I hope, a sufficient justification for reprinting it as it stands. At the same time, there are a number of points that seem to me to call for some further explanation, and I shall accordingly devote the remainder of this new introduction to commenting briefly upon them.

THE PRINCIPLE OF VERIFICATION

The principle of verification is supposed to furnish a criterion by which it can be determined whether or not a sentence is literally meaningful. A simple way to formulate it would be to say that a sentence had literal meaning if and only if the proposition it expressed was either analytic or empirically verifiable. To this, however, it might be objected that unless a sentence was literally meaningful it would not express a proposition;[1] for it is commonly assumed that every proposition is either true or false, and to say that a sentence expressed what was either true or false would entail saying that it was literally meaningful. Accordingly, if the principle of verification were formulated in

[1] Vide M. Lazerowitz, "The Principle of Verifiability," *Mind*, 1937, pp. 372–8.

5

this way, it might be argued not only that it was incomplete as a criterion of meaning, since it would not cover the case of sentences which did not express any propositions at all, but also that it was otiose, on the ground that the question which it was designed to answer must already have been answered before the principle could be applied. It will be seen that when I introduce the principle in this book I try to avoid this difficulty by speaking of "putative propositions" and of the proposition which a sentence "purports to express"; but this device is not satisfactory. For, in the first place, the use of words like "putative" and "purports" seems to bring in psychological considerations into which I do not wish to enter, and secondly, in the case where the "putative proposition" is neither analytic nor empirically verifiable, there would, according to this way of speaking, appear to be nothing that the sentence in question could properly be said to express. But if a sentence expresses nothing there seems to be a contradiction in saying that what it expresses is empirically unverifiable; for even if the sentence is adjudged on this ground to be meaningless, the reference to "what it expresses" appears still to imply that something is expressed.

This is, however, no more than a terminological difficulty, and there are various ways in which it might be met. One of them would be to make the criterion of verifiability apply directly to sentences, and so eliminate the reference to propositions altogether. This would, indeed, run counter to ordinary usage, since one would not normally say of a sentence, as opposed to a proposition, that it was capable of being verified, or, for that matter, that it was either true or false; but it might be argued that such a departure from ordinary usage was justified, if it could be shown to have some practical advantage. The fact is, however, that the practical advantage seems to lie on the other side. For while it is true.that the use of the word "proposition" does not enable us to say anything that we could not, in principle, say without it, it does fulfil an important function; for it makes it possible to express what is valid not merely for a particular sentence s but for any sentence to which s is logically equivalent. Thus, if I assert, for example, that the proposition p is entailed by the proposition q I am indeed claiming implicitly that the English sentence s which expresses p can be validly derived from the English sentence r which expresses q, but this is not

6

the whole of my claim. For, if I am right, it will also follow that any sentence, whether of the English or any other language, that is equivalent to *s* can be validly derived, in the language in question, from any sentence that is equivalent to *r*; and it is this that my use of the word "proposition" indicates. Admittedly, we could decide to use the word "sentence" in the way in which we now use the word "proposition," but this would not be conducive to clarity, particularly as the word "sentence" is already ambiguous. Thus, in a case of repetition, it can be said either that there are two different sentences or that the same sentence has been formulated twice. It is in the latter sense that I have so far been using the word, but the other usage is equally legitimate. In either usage, a sentence which was expressed in English would be accounted a different sentence from its French equivalent, but this would not hold good for the new usage of the word "sentence" that we should be introducing if we substituted "sentence" for "proposition." For in that case we should have to say that the English expression and its French equivalent were different formulations of the same sentence. We might indeed be justified in increasing the ambiguity of the word "sentence" in this way if we thereby avoided any of the difficulties that have been thought to be attached to the use of the word "proposition"; but I do not think that this is to be achieved by the mere substitution of one verbal token for another. Accordingly, I conclude that this technical use of the word "sentence," though legitimate in itself, would be likely to promote confusion, without securing us any compensatory advantage.

A second way of meeting our original difficulty would be to extend the use of the word "proposition," so that anything that could properly be called a sentence would be said to express a proposition, whether or not the sentence was literally meaningful. This course would have the advantage of simplicity, but it is open to two objections. The first is that it would involve a departure from current philosophical usage; and the second is that it would oblige us to give up the rule that every proposition is to be accounted either true or false. For while, if we adopted this new usage, we should still be able to say that anything that was either true or false was a proposition, the converse would no longer hold good; for a proposition would be neither true nor

7

false if it was expressed by a sentence which was literally meaningless. I do not myself think that these objections are very serious, but they are perhaps sufficiently so to make it advisable to solve our terminological problem in some other way.

The solution that I prefer is to introduce a new technical term; and for this purpose I shall make use of the familiar word "statement," though I shall perhaps be using it in a slightly unfamiliar sense. Thus I propose that any form of words that is grammatically significant shall be held to constitute a sentence, and that every indicative sentence, whether it is literally meaningful or not, shall be regarded as expressing a statement. Furthermore, any two sentences which are mutually translatable will be said to express the same statement. The word "proposition," on the other hand, will be reserved for what is expressed by sentences which are literally meaningful. Thus, the class of propositions becomes, in this usage, a sub-class of the class of statements, and one way of describing the use of the principle of verification would be to say that it provided a means of determining when an indicative sentence expressed a proposition, or, in other words, of distinguishing the statements that belonged to the class of propositions from those that did not.

It should be remarked that this decision to say that sentences express statements involves nothing more than the adoption of a verbal convention; and the proof of this is that the question, "What do sentences express?" to which it provides an answer is not a factual question. To ask of any particular sentence what it is that it expresses may, indeed, be to put a factual question; and one way of answering it would be to produce another sentence which was a translation of the first. But if the general question, "What do sentences express?" is to be interpreted factually, all that can be said in answer is that, since it is not the case that all sentences are equivalent, there is not any one thing that they all express. At the same time, it is useful to have a means of referring indefinitely to "what sentences express" in cases where the sentences themselves are not particularly specified; and this purpose is served by the introduction of the word "statement" as a technical term. Accordingly, in saying that sentences express statements, we are indicating how this technical term is to be understood, but we are not thereby conveying any factual information in the sense in which we should be conveying factual

8

information if the question we were answering was empirical. This may, indeed, seem a point too obvious to be worth making; but the question, "What do sentences express?" is closely analogous to the question, "What do sentences mean?" and, as I have tried to show elsewhere,[1] the question, "What do sentences mean?" has been a source of confusion to philosophers because they have mistakenly thought it to be factual. To say that indicative sentences mean propositions is indeed legitimate, just as it is legitimate to say that they express statements. But what we are doing, in giving answers of this kind, is to lay down conventional definitions; and it is important that these conventional definitions should not be confused with statements of empirical fact.

Returning now to the principle of verification, we may, for the sake of brevity, apply it directly to statements rather than to the sentences which express them, and we can then reformulate it by saying that a statement is held to be literally meaningful if and only if it is either analytic or empirically verifiable. But what is to be understood in this context by the term "verifiable"? I do indeed attempt to answer this question in the first chapter of this book; but I have to acknowledge that my answer is not very satisfactory.

To begin with, it will be seen that I distinguish between a "strong" and a "weak" sense of the term "verifiable," and that I explain this distinction by saying that "a proposition is said to be verifiable in the strong sense of the term, if and only if its truth could be conclusively established in experience," but that "it is verifiable, in the weak sense, if it is possible for experience to render it probable." And I then give reasons for deciding that it is only the weak sense of the term that is required by my principle of verification. What I seem, however, to have overlooked is that, as I represent them, these are not two genuine alternatives.[2] For I subsequently go on to argue that all empirical propositions are hypotheses which are continually subject to the test of further experience; and from this it would follow not merely that the truth of any such proposition never was conclusively established but that it never could be; for however

[1] In *The Foundations of Empirical Knowledge*, pp. 92–104.
[2] Vide M. Lazerowitz, "Strong and Weak Verification," *Mind*, 1939, pp. 202–13.

strong the evidence in its favour, there would never be a point at which it was impossible for further experience to go against it. But this would mean that my "strong" sense of the term "verifiable" had no possible application, and in that case there was no need for me to qualify the other sense of "verifiable" as weak; for on my own showing it was the only sense in which any proposition could conceivably be verified.

If I do not now draw this conclusion, it is because I have come to think that there is a class of empirical propositions of which it is permissible to say that they can be verified conclusively. It is characteristic of these propositions, which I have elsewhere[1] called "basic propositions," that they refer solely to the content of a single experience, and what may be said to verify them conclusively is the occurrence of the experience to which they uniquely refer. Furthermore, I should now agree with those who say that propositions of this kind are "incorrigible," assuming that what is meant by their being incorrigible is that it is impossible to be mistaken about them except in a verbal sense. In a verbal sense, indeed, it is always possible to misdescribe one's experience; but if one intends to do no more than record what is experienced without relating it to anything else, it is not possible to be factually mistaken; and the reason for this is that one is making no claim that any further fact could confute. It is, in short, a case of "nothing venture, nothing lose." It is, however, equally a case of "nothing venture, nothing win," since the mere recording of one's present experience does not serve to convey any information either to any other person or indeed to oneself; for in knowing a basic proposition to be true one obtains no further knowledge than what is already afforded by the occurrence of the relevant experience. Admittedly, the form of words that is used to express a basic proposition may be understood to express something that is informative both to another person and to oneself, but when it is so understood it no longer expresses a basic proposition. It was for this reason, indeed, that I maintained, in the fifth chapter of this book, that there could not be such things as basic propositions, in the sense in which I am now using the term; for the burden of my argument was that no synthetic proposition could be purely ostensive. My reasoning on

[1] "Verification and Experience," *Proceedings of the Aristotelian Society*, Vol. XXXVII; cf. also *The Foundations of Empirical Knowledge*, pp. 80–4.

this point was not in itself incorrect, but I think that I mistook its purport. For I seem not to have perceived that what I was really doing was to suggest a motive for refusing to apply the term "proposition" to statements that "directly recorded an immediate experience"; and this is a terminological point which is not of any great importance.

Whether or not one chooses to include basic statements in the class of empirical propositions, and so to admit that some empirical propositions can be conclusively verified, it will remain true that the vast majority of the propositions that people actually express are neither themselves basic statements, nor deducible from any finite set of basic statements. Consequently, if the principle of verification is to be seriously considered as a criterion of meaning, it must be interpreted in such a way as to admit statements that are not so strongly verifiable as basic statements are supposed to be. But how then is the word "verifiable" to be understood?

It will be seen that, in this book, I begin by suggesting that a statement is "weakly" verifiable, and therefore meaningful, according to my criterion, if "some possible sense-experience would be relevant to the determination of its truth or falsehood." But, as I recognize, this itself requires interpretation; for the word "relevant" is uncomfortably vague. Accordingly, I put forward a second version of my principle, which I shall restate here in slightly different terms, using the phrase "observation-statement," in place of "experiential proposition," to designate a statement "which records an actual or possible observation." In this version, then, the principle is that a statement is verifiable, and consequently meaningful, if some observation-statement can be deduced from it in conjunction with certain other premises, without being deducible from those other premises alone.

I say of this criterion that it "seems liberal enough," but in fact it is far too liberal, since it allows meaning to any statement whatsoever. For, given any statement "S" and an observation-statement "O," "O" follows from "S" and "if S then O" without following from "if S then O" alone. Thus, the statements "the Absolute is lazy" and "if the Absolute is lazy, this is white" jointly entail the observation-statement "this is white," and since "this is white" does not follow from either of these premises, taken by itself, both of them satisfy my criterion of meaning. Furthermore, this would hold good for any other piece of nonsense that one cared to put, as an example, in place of "the Absolute is lazy," provided only that it had the grammatical form of an indicative sentence. But a criterion of meaning that allows such latitude as this is evidently unacceptable.[1]

It may be remarked that the same objection applies to the proposal that we should take the possibility of falsification as our criterion. For, given any statement "S" and any observation-statement "O", "O" will be incompatible with the conjunction of "S" and "if S then not O." We could indeed avoid the difficulty, in either case, by leaving out the stipulation about the other premises. But as this would involve the exclusion of all hypotheticals from the class of empirical propositions, we should escape from making our criteria too liberal only at the cost of making them too stringent.

Another difficulty which I overlooked in my original attempt to formulate the principle of verification is that most empirical propositions are in some degree vague. Thus, as I have remarked elsewhere,[2] what is required to verify a statement about a material thing is never the occurrence of precisely this or precisely that sense-content, but only the occurrence of one or other of the sense-contents that fall within a fairly indefinite range. We do indeed test any such statement by making observations which consist in the occurrence of particular sense-contents; but, for any test that we actually carry out, there is always an indefinite number of other tests, differing to some extent in respect either of their conditions or their results, that would have served the same purpose. And this means that there is never any set of observation-statements of which it can truly be said that precisely they are entailed by any given statement about a material thing.

Nevertheless, it is only by the occurrence of some sense-content, and consequently by the truth of some observation-statement, that any statement about a material thing is actually verified; and from this it follows that every significant statement about a material thing can be represented as entailing a disjunction of observation-statements, although the terms of this disjunction,

---

[1] Vide I. Berlin, "Verifiability in Principle," *Proceedings of the Aristotelian Society*, Vol. XXXIX.

[2] *The Foundations of Empirical Knowledge*, pp. 240–1.

being infinite, can not be enumerated in detail. Consequently, I do not think that we need be troubled by the difficulty about vagueness, so long as it is understood that when we speak of the "entailment" of observation-statements, what we are considering to be deducible from the premises in question is not any particular observation-statement, but only one or other of a set of such statements, where the defining characteristic of the set is that all its members refer to sense-contents that fall within a certain specifiable range.

There remains the more serious objection that my criterion, as it stands, allows meaning to any indicative statement whatsoever. To meet this, I shall emend it as follows. I propose to say that a statement is directly verifiable if it is either itself an observation-statement, or is such that in conjunction with one or more observation-statements it entails at least one observation-statement which is not deducible from these other premises alone; and I propose to say that a statement is indirectly verifiable if it satisfies the following conditions: first, that in conjunction with certain other premises it entails one or more directly verifiable statements which are not deducible from these other premises alone; and secondly, that these other premises do not include any statement that is not either analytic, or directly verifiable, or capable of being independently established as indirectly verifiable. And I can now reformulate the principle of verification as requiring of a literally meaningful statement, which is not analytic, that it should be either directly or indirectly verifiable, in the foregoing sense.

It may be remarked that in giving my account of the conditions in which a statement is to be considered indirectly verifiable, I have explicitly put in the proviso that the "other premises" may include analytic statements; and my reason for doing this is that I intend in this way to allow for the case of scientific theories which are expressed in terms that do not themselves designate anything observable. For while the statements that contain these terms may not appear to describe anything that anyone could ever observe, a "dictionary" may be provided by means of which they can be transformed into statements that are verifiable; and the statements which constitute the dictionary can be regarded as analytic. Were this not so, there would be nothing to choose between such scientific theories and those that I should dismiss as metaphysical; but I take it to be characteristic of the metaphysician, in my somewhat pejorative sense of the term, not only that his statements do not describe anything that is capable, even in principle, of being observed, but also that no dictionary is provided by means of which they can be transformed into statements that are directly or indirectly verifiable.

Metaphysical statements, in my sense of the term, are excluded also by the older empiricist principle that no statement is literally meaningful unless it describes what could be experienced, where the criterion of what could be experienced is that it should be something of the same kind as actually has been experienced.[1] But, apart from its lack of precision, this empiricist principle has, to my mind, the defect of imposing too harsh a condition upon the form of scientific theories; for it would seem to imply that it was illegitimate to introduce any term that did not itself designate something observable. The principle of verification, on the other hand, is, as I have tried to show, more liberal in this respect, and in view of the use that is actually made of scientific theories which the other would rule out, I think that the more liberal criterion is to be preferred.

It has sometimes been assumed by my critics that I take the principle of verification to imply that no statement can be evidence for another unless it is a part of its meaning; but this is not the case. Thus, to make use of a simple illustration, the statement that I have blood on my coat may, in certain circumstances, confirm the hypothesis that I have committed a murder, but it is not part of the meaning of the statement that I have committed a murder that I should have blood upon my coat, nor, as I understand it, does the principle of verification imply that it is. For one statement may be evidence for another, and still neither itself express a necessary condition of the truth of this other statement, nor belong to any set of statements which determines a range within which such a necessary condition falls; and it is only in

[1] cf. Bertrand Russell, *The Problems of Philosophy*, p. 91: "Every proposition which we can understand must be composed wholly of constituents with which we are acquainted." And, if I understand him correctly, this is what Professor W. T. Stace has in mind when he speaks of a "Principle of Observable Kinds." Vide his "Positivism," *Mind*, 1944. Stace argues that the principle of verification "rests upon" the principle of observable kinds, but this is a mistake. It is true that every statement that is allowed to be meaningful by the principle of observable kinds is also allowed to be meaningful by the principle of verification: but the converse does not hold.

these cases that the principle of verification yields the conclusion that the one statement is part of the meaning of the other. Thus, from the fact that it is only by the making of some observation that any statement about a material thing can be directly verified it follows, according to the principle of verification, that every such statement contains some observation-statement or other as part of its meaning, and it follows also that, although its generality may prevent any finite set of observation-statements from exhausting its meaning, it does not contain anything as part of its meaning that cannot be represented as an observation-statement; but there may still be many observation-statements that are relevant to its truth or falsehood without being part of its meaning at all. Again, a person who affirms the existence of a deity may try to support his contention by appealing to the facts of religious experience; but it does not follow from this that the factual meaning of his statement is wholly contained in the propositions by which these religious experiences are described. For there may be other empirical facts that he would also consider to be relevant; and it is possible that the descriptions of these other empirical facts can more properly be regarded as containing the factual meaning of his statement than the descriptions of the religious experiences. At the same time, if one accepts the principle of verification, one must hold that his statement does not have any other factual meaning than what is contained in at least some of the relevant empirical propositions; and that if it is so interpreted that no possible experience could go to verify it, it does not have any factual meaning at all.

In putting forward the principle of verification as a criterion of meaning, I do not overlook the fact that the word "meaning" is commonly used in a variety of senses, and I do not wish to deny that in some of these senses a statement may properly be said to be meaningful even though it is neither analytic nor empirically verifiable. I should, however, claim that there was at least one proper use of the word "meaning" in which it would be incorrect to say that a statement was meaningful unless it satisfied the principle of verification; and I have, perhaps tendentiously, used the expression "literal meaning" to distinguish this use from the others, while applying the expression "factual meaning" to the case of statements which satisfy my criterion without being analytic. Furthermore, I suggest that it is only if it is literally meaningful, in this sense, that a statement can properly be said to be either true or false. Thus, while I wish the principle of verification itself to be regarded, not as an empirical hypothesis,[1] but as a definition, it is not supposed to be entirely arbitrary. It is indeed open to anyone to adopt a different criterion of meaning and so to produce an alternative definition which may very well correspond to one of the ways in which the word "meaning" is commonly used. And if a statement satisfied such a criterion, there is, no doubt, some proper use of the word "understanding" in which it would be capable of being understood. Nevertheless, I think that, unless it satisfied the principle of verification, it would not be capable of being understood in the sense in which either scientific hypotheses or common-sense statements are habitually understood. I confess, however, that it now seems to me unlikely that any metaphysician would yield to a claim of this kind; and although I should still defend the use of the criterion of verifiability as a methodological principle, I realize that for the effective elimination of metaphysics it needs to be supported by detailed analyses of particular metaphysical arguments.

THE "A PRIORI"

In saying that the certainty of *a priori* propositions depends upon the fact that they are tautologies, I use the word "tautology" in such a way that a proposition can be said to be a tautology if it is analytic; and I hold that a proposition is analytic if it is true solely in virtue of the meaning of its constituent symbols, and cannot therefore be either confirmed or refuted by any fact of experience. It has, indeed, been suggested[2] that my treatment of *a priori* propositions makes them into a sub-class of empirical propositions. For I sometimes seem to imply that they describe the way in which certain symbols are used, and it is undoubtedly an empirical fact that people use symbols in the ways that they do. This is not, however, the position that I wish to hold; nor do I think that I am committed to it. For although I say that the validity of *a priori* propositions depends upon certain facts about verbal usage, I do not think that this is

[1] Both Dr. A. C. Ewing, "Meaninglessness," *Mind*, 1937, pp. 347–64, and Stace, *op. cit.*, take it to be an empirical hypothesis.

[2] e.g. by Professor C. D. Broad, "Are these Synthetic *a priori* Truths," *Supplementary Proceedings of the Aristotelian Society*, Vol. XV.

equivalent to saying that they describe these facts in the sense in which empirical propositions may describe the facts that verify them; and indeed I argue that they do not, in this sense, describe any facts at all. At the same time I allow that the usefulness of *a priori* propositions is founded both on the empirical fact that certain symbols are used in the way that they are and on the empirical fact that the symbols in question are successfully applied to our experience; and I try in the fourth chapter of this book to show how this is so.

Just as it is a mistake to identify *a priori* propositions with empirical propositions about language, so I now think that it is a mistake to say that they are themselves linguistic rules.[1] For apart from the fact that they can properly be said to be true, which linguistic rules cannot, they are distinguished also by being necessary, whereas linguistic rules are arbitrary. At the same time, if they are necessary it is only because the relevant linguistic rules are presupposed. Thus, it is a contingent, empirical fact that the word "earlier" is used in English to mean earlier, and it is an arbitrary, though convenient, rule of language that words that stand for temporal relations are to be used transitively; but, given this rule, the proposition that, if A is earlier than B and B is earlier than C, A is earlier than C becomes a necessary truth. Similarly, in Russell's and Whitehead's system of logic, it is a contingent, empirical fact that the sign " ⊃ " should have been given the meaning that it has, and the rules which govern the use of this sign are conventions, which themselves are neither true nor false; but, given these rules the *a priori* proposition "q. ⊃ .p ⊃ q" is necessarily true. Being *a priori*, this proposition gives no information in the ordinary sense in which an empirical proposition may be said to give information, nor does it itself prescribe how the logical constant " ⊃ " is to be used. What it does is to elucidate the proper use of this logical constant; and it is in this way that it is informative.

An argument which has been brought against the doctrine that *a priori* propositions of the form "p entails q" are analytic is that it is possible for one proposition to entail another without containing it as part of its meaning; for it is assumed that this would not be possible if the analytic view of entailment were

[1] This contradicts what I said in my contribution to a symposium on "Truth by Convention," *Analysis*, Vol. 4, Nos. 2 and 3; cf. also Norman Malcolm, "Are Necessary Propositions really Verbal," *Mind*, 1940, pp. 189–203.

correct.[1] But the answer to this is that the question whether one proposition is part of the meaning of another is ambiguous. If you say, for example, as I think most of those who raise this objection would, that q is not part of the meaning of p if it is possible to understand p without thinking of q, then clearly one proposition can entail another without containing it as part of its meaning; for it can hardly be maintained that anyone who considers a given set of propositions must be immediately conscious of all that they entail. This is, however, to make a point with which I do not think that any upholder of the analytic view of entailment would wish to disagree; for it is common ground that deductive reasoning may lead to conclusions which are new in the sense that one had not previously apprehended them. But if this is admitted by those who say that propositions of the form "p entails q" are analytic, how can they also say that if p entails q the meaning of q is contained in that of p? The answer is that they are using a criterion of meaning, whether the verification principle or another, from which it follows that when one proposition entails another the meaning of the second is contained in that of the first. In other words, they determine the meaning of a proposition by considering what it entails; and this is, to my mind, a perfectly legitimate procedure.[2] If this procedure is adopted the proposition that, if p entails q, the meaning of q is contained in that of p, itself becomes analytic; and it is therefore not to be refuted by any such psychological facts as those on which the critics of this view rely. At the same time, it may fairly be objected to it that it does not give us much information about the nature of entailment; for although it entitles us to say that the logical consequences of a proposition are explicative of its meaning, this is only because the meaning of a proposition is understood to depend upon what it entails.

PROPOSITIONS ABOUT THE PAST AND ABOUT OTHER MINDS

By saying of propositions about the past that they are "rules for the prediction of those 'historical' experiences which are

[1] Vide A. C. Ewing, "The Linguistic Theory of *a priori* Propositions," *Proceedings of the Aristotelian Society*, 1940; cf. also Professor G. E. Moore, "A Reply to My Critics," *The Philosophy of G. E. Moore*, pp. 575–6, and Professor E. Nagel's review of *The Philosophy of G. E. Moore*, *Mind*, 1944, p. 64.

[2] cf. Norman Malcolm, "The Nature of Entailment," *Mind*, 1940, pp. 333–47.

commonly said to verify them" I seem to imply that they can somehow be translated into propositions about present or future experiences. But this is certainly incorrect. Statements about the past may be verifiable in the sense that when they are conjoined with other premises of a suitable kind they may entail observation-statements which do not follow from these other premises alone; but I do not think that the truth of any observation-statements which refer to the present or the future is a necessary condition of the truth of any statement about the past. This does not mean, however, that propositions referring to the past cannot be analysed in phenomenal terms; for they can be taken as implying that certain observations would have occurred if certain conditions had been fulfilled. But the trouble is that these conditions never can be fulfilled; for they require of the observer that he should occupy a temporal position that *ex hypothesi* he does not. This difficulty, however, is not a peculiarity of propositions about the past; for it is true also of unfulfilled conditionals about the present that their protases cannot in fact be satisfied, since they require of the observer that he should be occupying a different spatial position from that which he actually does. But, as I have remarked elsewhere,[1] just as it is a contingent fact that a person happens at a given moment to be occupying a particular position in space, so is it a contingent fact that he happens to be living at a particular time. And from this I conclude that if one is justified in saying that events which are remote in space are observable, in principle, the same may be said of events which are situated in the past.

Concerning the experiences of others I confess that I am doubtful whether the account that is given in this book is correct; but I am not convinced that it is not. In another work, I have argued that, since it is a contingent fact that any particular experience belongs to the series of experiences which constitutes a given person, rather than to another series which constitutes someone else, there is a sense in which "it is not logically inconceivable that I should have an experience that is in fact owned by someone else"; and from this I inferred that the use of "the argument from analogy" might after all be justified.[2] More

---

[1] *The Foundations of Empirical Knowledge*, p. 167; cf. also Professor G. Ryle, "Unverifiability by Me," *Analysis*, Vol. 4, No. 1.

[2] *The Foundations of Empirical Knowledge*, pp. 168–70.

recently, however, I have come to think that this reasoning is very dubious. For while it is possible to imagine circumstances in which we might have found it convenient to say of two different persons that they owned the same experience, the fact is that, according to our present usage, it is a necessary proposition that they do not; and, since this is so, I am afraid that the argument from analogy remains open to the objections that are brought against it in this book. Consequently, I am inclined to revert to a "behaviouristic" interpretation of propositions about other people's experiences. But I own that it has an air of paradox which prevents me from being wholly confident that it is true.[1]

THE EMOTIVE THEORY OF VALUES

The emotive theory of values, which is developed in the sixth chapter of this book, has provoked a fair amount of criticism; but I find that this criticism has been directed more often against the positivistic principles on which the theory has been assumed to depend than against the theory itself.[2] Now I do not deny that in putting forward this theory I was concerned with maintaining the general consistency of my position; but it is not the only ethical theory that would have satisfied this requirement, nor does it actually entail any of the non-ethical statements which form the remainder of my argument. Consequently, even if it could be shown that these other statements were invalid, this would not in itself refute the emotive analysis of ethical judgements; and in fact I believe this analysis to be valid on its own account.

Having said this, I must acknowledge that the theory is here presented in a very summary way, and that it needs to be supported by a more detailed analysis of specimen ethical judgements than I make any attempt to give.[3] Thus, among other

[1] My confidence in it has been somewhat increased by John Wisdom's interesting series of articles on "Other Minds," *Mind*, 1940–3. But I am not sure that this is the effect that he intended them to produce.

[2] cf. Sir W. David Ross, *The Foundations of Ethics*, pp. 30–41.

[3] I understand that this deficiency has been made good by C. L. Stevenson in his book, *Ethics and Language*, but the book was published in America and I have not yet been able to obtain it. There is a review of it by Austin Duncan-Jones in *Mind*, October, 1945, and a good indication of Stevenson's line of argument is to be found in his articles on "The Emotive Meaning of Ethical Terms," *Mind*, 1937, "Ethical Judgements and Avoidability," *Mind*, 1938, and "Persuasive Definitions," *Mind*, 1938.

things, I fail to bring out the point that the common objects of moral approval or disapproval are not particular actions so much as classes of actions; by which I mean that if an action is labelled right or wrong, or good or bad, as the case may be, it is because it is thought to be an action of a certain type. And this point seems to me important, because I think that what seems to be an ethical judgement is very often a factual classification of an action as belonging to some class of actions by which a certain moral attitude on the part of the speaker is habitually aroused. Thus, a man who is a convinced utilitarian may simply mean by calling an action right that it tends to promote, or more probably that it is the sort of action that tends to promote, the general happiness; and in that case the validity of his statement becomes an empirical matter of fact. Similarly, a man who bases his ethical upon his religious views may actually mean by calling an action right or wrong that it is the sort of action that is enjoined or forbidden by some ecclesiastical authority; and this also may be empirically verified. Now in these cases the form of words by which the factual statement is expressed is the same as that which would be used to express a normative statement; and this may to some extent explain why statements which are recognized to be normative are nevertheless often thought to be factual. Moreover, a great many ethical statements contain, as a factual element, some description of the action, or the situation, to which the ethical term in question is being applied. But although there may be a number of cases in which this ethical term is itself to be understood descriptively, I do not think that this is always so. I think that there are many statements in which an ethical term is used in a purely normative way, and it is to statements of this kind that the emotive theory of ethics is intended to apply.

The objection that if the emotive theory was correct it would be impossible for one person to contradict another on a question of value is here met by the answer that what seem to be disputes about questions of value are really disputes about questions of fact. I should, however, have made it clear that it does not follow from this that two persons cannot significantly disagree about a question of value, or that it is idle for them to attempt to convince one another. For a consideration of any dispute about a matter of taste will show that there can be disagreement without formal contradiction, and that in order to alter another man's opinions, in the sense of getting him to change his attitude, it is not necessary to contradict anything that he asserts. Thus, if one wishes to affect another person in such a way as to bring his sentiments on a given point into accordance with one's own, there are various ways in which one may proceed. One may, for example, call his attention to certain facts that one supposes him to have overlooked; and, as I have already remarked, I believe that much of what passes for ethical discussion is a proceeding of this type. It is, however, also possible to influence other people by a suitable choice of emotive language; and this is the practical justification for the use of normative expressions of value. At the same time, it must be admitted that if the other person persists in maintaining his contrary attitude, without however disputing any of the relevant facts, a point is reached at which the discussion can go no further. And in that case there is no sense in asking which of the conflicting views is true. For, since the expression of a value judgement is not a proposition, the question of truth or falsehood does not here arise.

THE NATURE OF PHILOSOPHICAL ANALYSIS

In citing Bertrand Russell's theory of descriptions as a specimen of philosophical analysis, I unfortunately made a mistake in my exposition of the theory. For, having taken the familiar example of "The author of *Waverley* was Scotch," I said that it was equivalent to "One person, and one person only, wrote *Waverley*, and that person was Scotch." But, as Professor Stebbing pointed out in her review of this book, "if the word 'that' is used referentially, then 'that person was Scotch' is equivalent to the whole of the original," and if it is used demonstratively, then the defining expression "is not a translation of the original."[1] The version sometimes given by Russell himself[2] is that "The author of *Waverley* was Scotch" is equivalent to a conjunction of the three propositions "At least one person wrote *Waverley*"; "At most one person wrote *Waverley*"; and "Whoever wrote *Waverley* was Scotch." Professor Moore, however, has remarked[3] that if the

[1] *Mind*, 1936, p. 358.

[2] e.g. in his *Introduction to Mathematical Philosophy*, pp. 172–80.

[3] In an article on "Russell's Theory of Descriptions," *The Philosophy of Bertrand Russell*, vide especially pp. 179–89.

words "whoever wrote *Waverley*" are understood "in the most natural way," the first of these propositions is superfluous; for he argues that part of what would ordinarily be meant by saying that whoever wrote *Waverley* was Scotch is that somebody did write *Waverley*. Accordingly, he suggests that the proposition which Russell intended to express by the words "whoever wrote *Waverley* was Scotch" is "one which can be expressed more clearly by the words 'There never was a person who wrote *Waverley* but was not Scotch.' " And even so he does not think that the proposed translation is correct. For he objects that to say of someone that he is the author of a work does not entail saying that he wrote it, since if he had composed it without actually writing it down he could still properly be called its author. To this Russell has replied that it was "the inevitable vagueness and ambiguity of any language used for every-day purposes" that led him to use an artificial symbolic language in *Principia Mathematica*, and that it is in the definitions given in *Principia Mathematica* that the whole of his theory of descriptions consists.[1] In saying this, however, he is, I think, unjust to himself. For it seems to me that one of the great merits of his theory of descriptions is that it does throw light upon the use of a certain class of expressions in ordinary speech, and that this is a point of philosophical importance. For, by showing that expressions like "the present King of France" do not function as names, the theory exposes the fallacy that has led philosophers to believe in "subsistent entities." Thus, while it is unfortunate that the example most frequently chosen to illustrate the theory should contain a minor inaccuracy, I do not think that this seriously affects its value, even in its application to every-day language. For, as I point out in this book, the object of analysing "The author of *Waverley* was Scotch" is not just to obtain an accurate translation of this particular sentence, but to elucidate the use of a whole class of expressions, of which "the author of *Waverley*" serves merely as a typical example.

A more serious mistake than my misrendering of "The author of *Waverley* was Scotch" was my assumption that philosophical analysis consisted mainly in the provision of "definitions in use." It is, indeed, true that what I describe as philosophical analysis is very largely a matter of exhibiting the inter-relationship of

[1] "Reply to Criticisms," *The Philosophy of Bertrand Russell*, p. 690.

different types of propositions;[1] but the cases in which this process actually yields a set of definitions are the exception rather than the rule. Thus the problem of showing how statements about material things are related to observation-statements, which is, in effect, the traditional problem of perception, might be thought to require for its solution that one should indicate a method of translating statements about material things into observation-statements, and thereby furnish what could be regarded as a definition of a material thing. But, in fact, this is impossible; for, as I have already remarked, no finite set of observation statements is ever equivalent to a statement about a material thing. What one can do, however, is to construct a schema which shows what sort of relations must obtain between sense-contents for it to be true, in any given case, that a material thing exists: and while this process cannot, properly speaking, be said to yield a definition, it does have the effect of showing how the one type of statement is related to the other.[2] Similarly, in the field of political philosophy, one will probably not be able to translate statements on the political level into statements about individual persons; for although what is said about a State, for example, is to be verified only by the behaviour of certain individuals, such a statement is usually indefinite in a way that prevents any particular set of statements about the behaviour of individuals from being exactly equivalent to it. Nevertheless, here again it is possible to indicate what types of relations must obtain between individual persons for the political statements in question to be true: so that even if no actual definitions are obtained, the meaning of the political statements is appropriately clarified.

In such cases as these one does indeed arrive at something that approaches a definition in use; but there are other cases of philosophical analysis in which nothing even approaching a definition is either provided or sought. Thus, when Professor Moore suggests that to say that "existence is not a predicate" may be a way of saying that "there is some very important difference between the way in which 'exist' is used in such a sentence as

---

[1] G. Ryle, *Philosophical Arguments*, Inaugural Lecture delivered before the University of Oxford, 1945.

[2] Vide *The Foundations of Empirical Knowledge*, pp. 243–63; and R. B. Braithwaite, "Propositions about Material Objects," *Proceedings of the Aristotelian Society*, Vol. XXXVIII.

'Tame tigers exist' and the way in which 'growl' is used in 'Tame tigers growl,' " he does not develop his point by giving rules for the translation of one set of sentences into another. What he does is to remark that whereas it makes good sense to say "All tame tigers growl" or "Most tame tigers growl" it would be nonsense to say "All tame tigers exist" or "Most tame tigers exist."[1] Now this may seem a rather trivial point for him to make, but in fact it is philosophically illuminating. For it is precisely the assumption that existence is a predicate that gives plausibility to "the ontological argument"; and the ontological argument is supposed to demonstrate the existence of a God. Consequently Moore by pointing out a peculiarity in the use of the word "exist" helps to protect us from a serious fallacy; so that his procedure, though different from that which Russell follows in his theory of descriptions, tends to achieve the same philosophical end.[2]

I maintain in this book that it is not within the province of philosophy to justify our scientific or common-sense beliefs; for their validity is an empirical matter, which cannot be settled by *a priori* means. At the same time, the question of what constitutes such a justification is philosophical, as the existence of "the problem of induction" shows. Here again, what is required is not necessarily a definition. For although I believe that the problems connected with induction can be reduced to the question of what is meant by saying that one proposition is good evidence for another, I doubt if the way to answer this is to construct a formal definition of "evidence." What is chiefly wanted, I think, is an analysis of scientific method, and although it might be possible to express the results of this analysis in the form of definitions, this would not be an achievement of primary importance. And here I may add that the reduction of philosophy to analysis need not be incompatible with the view that its function is to bring to light "the presuppositions of science." For if there are such presuppositions, they can no doubt be shown to be

[1] G. E. Moore, "Is Existence a Predicate?" *Supplementary Proceedings of the Aristotelian Society*, 1936. I have made use of the same illustration in my paper on "Does Philosophy analyse Common Sense?" symposium with A. E. Duncan-Jones, *Supplementary Proceedings of the Aristotelian Society*, 1937.

[2] I do not wish to imply that Moore himself was solely, or even primarily, concerned with refuting the ontological argument. But I think that his reasoning does achieve this, though not this alone. Similarly Russell's "theory of descriptions" has other uses besides relieving us of "subsistent entities,"

logically involved in the applications of scientific method, or in the use of certain scientific terms.

It used to be said by positivists of the Viennese school that the function of philosophy was not to put forward a special set of "philosophical" propositions, but to make other propositions clear; and this statement has at least the merit of bringing out the point that philosophy is not a source of speculative truth. Nevertheless I now think that it is incorrect to say that there are no philosophical propositions. For, whether they are true or false, the propositions that are expressed in such a book as this do fall into a special category; and since they are the sort of propositions that are asserted or denied by philosophers, I do not see why they should not be called philosophical. To say of them that they are, in some sense, about the usage of words, is, I believe, correct but also inadequate; for certainly not every statement about the usage of words is philosophical.[1] Thus, a lexicographer also seeks to give information about the usage of words, but the philosopher differs from him in being concerned, as I have tried to indicate, not with the use of particular expressions but with classes of expressions; and whereas the propositions of the lexicographer are empirical, philosophical propositions, if they are true, are usually analytic.[2] For the rest I can find no better way of explaining my conception of philosophy than by referring to examples; and one such example is the argument of this book.

A. J. AYER.

Wadham College, Oxford.
January, 1946.

[1] Vide "Does Philosophy analyse Common Sense?" and Duncan-Jones' paper on the same subject, *Supplementary Proceedings of the Aristotelian Society*, 1937; cf. also John Wisdom, "Metaphysics and Verification," *Mind*, 1938, and "Philosophy, Anxiety and Novelty," *Mind*, 1944.

[2] I have put in the qualifying word "usually" because I think that some empirical propositions, such as those that occur in histories of philosophy, may be counted as philosophical. And philosophers use empirical propositions as examples, to serve philosophical ends. But, in so far as they are not merely historical, I think that the truths discoverable by philosophical methods are analytic. At the same time I should add that the philosopher's business, as Professor Ryle has pointed out to me, is rather to "solve puzzles" than to discover truths.

CONTENTS

p. 33: What is the purpose and method of philosophy? Rejection of the metaphysical thesis that philosophy affords us knowledge of a transcendent reality. *34:* Kant also rejected metaphysics in this sense, but whereas he accused metaphysicians of ignoring the limits of the human understanding we accuse them of disobeying the rules which govern the significant use of language. *35:* Adoption of verifiability as a criterion for testing the significance of putative statements of fact. *36:* Distinction between conclusive and partial verification. No propositions can be conclusively verified. *38:* Or conclusively confuted. *38:* For a statement of fact to be genuine some possible observations must be relevant to the determination of its truth or falsehood. *39:* Examples of the kinds of assertions, familiar to philosophers, which are ruled out by our criterion. *41:* Metaphysical sentences defined as sentences which express neither tautologies nor empirical hypotheses. *42:* Linguistic confusions the prime source of metaphysics. *44:* Metaphysics and Poetry.

p. 46: Philosophy is not a search for first principles. *46:* Barrenness of Descartes' procedure. *48:* The function of philosophy is wholly critical. But this does not mean that it can give an *a priori* justification of our scientific or common-sense assumptions. *49:* There is no genuine problem of induction, as ordinarily conceived. *51:* Philosophising is an activity of analysis. *51:* Most of those who are commonly thought to have been great philosophers were philosophers in our sense, rather than metaphysicians. *52:* Locke, Berkeley, Hume as analysts. *53:* We adopt Berkeley's phenomenalism without his theism. *54:* And take a Humean view of causation. *56:* Philosophy in our sense is wholly independent of metaphysics. We are not committed to any doctrine of atomism. *57:* The philosopher as an analyst is not concerned with the physical properties of things, but only with the way in which we speak about them. *58:* Linguistic propositions disguised in factual terminology. *59:* Philosophy issues in definitions.

p. 59: Philosophy provides not *explicit* definitions, such as are given in dictionaries, but definitions *in use*. Explanation of this distinction. *60:* Russell's "theory of descriptions" as an example of philosophical analysis. *62:* Definition of an ambiguous symbol. *63:* Definition of a logical construction. *64:* Material things are logical constructions out of sense-contents. *64:* By defining the notion of a material thing in terms of sense-contents we solve the so-called problem of perception. *65:* A solution of this problem outlined as a further example of philosophical analysis. *68:* Utility of such analyses. *68:* Danger of saying that philosophy is concerned with meaning. *70:* The propositions of philosophy are not empirical propositions concerning the way in which people actually use words. They are concerned with the logical consequences of linguistic conventions. *71:* Rejection of the view that "every language has a structure concerning which *in the language* nothing can be said."

Ch. IV. The *A Priori*   *p.* 71

p. 71: As empiricists, we must deny that any general proposition concerning a matter of fact can be known certainly to be valid. *72:* How then are we to deal with the propositions of formal logic and mathematics? *74:* Rejection of Mill's view that these propositions are inductive generalisations. *77:* They are necessarily true because they are analytic. *77:* Kant's definitions of analytic and synthetic judgements. *78:* Emendation of Kant's definitions. *79:* Analytic propositions are tautological; they say nothing concerning any matter of fact. *80:* But they give us new knowledge, inasmuch as they bring to light the implications of our linguistic usages. *81:* Logic does not describe "the laws of thought." *82:* Nor geometry the properties of physical space. *84:* Our account of *a priori* truths undermines Kant's transcendental system. *85:* How, if they are tautological, can there be in mathematics and logic the possibility of invention and discovery?

Ch. V. Truth and Probability   *p.* 87

p. 87: What is truth? *88:* Definition of a proposition. *88:* The words "true" and "false" function in the sentence simply as assertion and negation signs. *90:* The "problem of truth" reduced to the question, How are propositions validated? *90:* The criterion of the validity of empirical propositions is not purely formal. *91:* No empirical propositions are certain, not even those which refer to immediate experience. *94:* Observation confirms or discredits not just a single hypothesis but a system of hypotheses. *95:* The "facts of experience" can never compel us to abandon a hypothesis. *96:* Danger of mistaking synthetic for analytic propositions. *97:* Hypotheses as rules which govern our expectation of future experience. *100:* Definition of rationality. *101:* Definition of probability in terms of rationality. *101:* Propositions referring to the past.

Ch. VI. Critique of Ethics and Theology   *p.* 102

p. 102: How does an empiricist deal with assertions of value? *103:* Distinction between various types of ethical enquiry. *104:* Utilitarian and subjectivist theories of ethics consistent with empiricism. *105:* But unacceptable on other grounds. *105:* Distinction between normative and descriptive ethical symbols. *106:* Rejection of intuitionism. *107:* Assertions of value are not scientific but "emotive." *107:* They are therefore neither true nor false. *108:* They are partly expressions of feeling, partly commands. *109:* Distinction between expressions and assertions of feeling. *110:* Objection that this view makes it impossible to dispute about questions of value. *110:* Actually, we never do dispute about questions of value, but always about questions of fact. *112:* Ethics as a branch of knowledge comprehended in the social sciences.

PREFACE TO FIRST EDITION

THE VIEWS which are put forward in this treatise derive from the doctrines of Bertrand Russell and Wittgenstein, which are themselves the logical outcome of the empiricism of Berkeley and David Hume. Like Hume, I divide all genuine propositions into two classes: those which, in his terminology, concern "relations of ideas," and those which concern "matters of fact." The former class comprises the *a priori* propositions of logic and pure mathematics, and these I allow to be necessary and certain only because they are analytic. That is, I maintain that the reason why these propositions cannot be confuted in experience is that they do not make any assertion about the empirical world, but simply record our determination to use symbols in a certain fashion. Propositions concerning empirical matters of fact, on the other hand, I hold to be hypotheses, which can be probable but never certain. And in giving an account of the method of their validation I claim also to have explained the nature of truth.

To test whether a sentence expresses a genuine empirical hypothesis, I adopt what may be called a modified verification principle. For I require of an empirical hypothesis, not indeed that it should be conclusively verifiable, but that some possible sense-experience should be relevant to the determination of its truth or falsehood. If a putative proposition fails to satisfy this principle, and is not a tautology, then I hold that it is metaphysical, and that, being metaphysical, it is neither true nor false but literally senseless. It will be found that much of what ordinarily passes for philosophy is metaphysical according to this criterion, and, in particular, that it can not be significantly asserted that there is a non-empirical world of values, or that men have immortal souls, or that there is a transcendent God.

As for the propositions of philosophy themselves, they are held to be linguistically necessary, and so analytic. And with regard to the relationship of philosophy and empirical science, it is, shown that the philosopher is not in a position to furnish speculative truths, which would, as it were, compete with the hypotheses of science, nor yet to pass *a priori* judgements upon the validity of scientific theories, but that his function is to clarify the propositions of science by exhibiting their logical relationships, and by defining the symbols which occur in them. Consequently I maintain that there is nothing in the nature of philosophy to warrant the existence of conflicting philosophical "schools." And I attempt to substantiate this by providing a definitive solution of the problems which have been the chief sources of controversy between philosophers in the past.

The view that philosophizing is an activity of analysis is associated in England with the work of G. E. Moore and his disciples. But while I have learned a great deal from Professor Moore, I have reason to believe that he and his followers are not prepared to adopt such a thoroughgoing phenomenalism as I do, and that they take a rather different view of the nature of philosophical analysis. The philosophers with whom I am in the closest agreement are those who compose the "Viennese circle," under the leadership of Moritz Schlick, and are commonly known as logical positivists. And of these I owe most to Rudolf Carnap. Further, I wish to acknowledge my indebtedness to Gilbert Ryle, my original tutor in philosophy, and to Isaiah Berlin, who have discussed with me every point in the argument of this treatise, and made many valuable suggestions, although they both disagree with much of what I assert. And I must also express my thanks to J. R. M. Willis for his correction of the proofs.

A. J. Ayer.

11 Foubert's Place,
  London.
    July 1935.

CHAPTER I

THE ELIMINATION OF METAPHYSICS

THE TRADITIONAL DISPUTES of philosophers are, for the most part, as unwarranted as they are unfruitful. The surest way to end them is to establish beyond question what should be the purpose and method of a philosophical enquiry. And this is by no means so difficult a task as the history of philosophy would lead one to suppose. For if there are any questions which science leaves it to philosophy to answer, a straightforward process of elimination must lead to their discovery.

We may begin by criticising the metaphysical thesis that philosophy affords us knowledge of a reality transcending the world of science and common sense. Later on, when we come to define metaphysics and account for its existence, we shall find that it is possible to be a metaphysician without believing in a transcendent reality; for we shall see that many metaphysical utterances are due to the commission of logical errors, rather than to a conscious desire on the part of their authors to go beyond the limits of experience. But it is convenient for us to take the case of those who believe that it is possible to have knowledge of a transcendent reality as a starting-point for our discussion. The arguments which we use to refute them will subsequently be found to apply to the whole of metaphysics.

One way of attacking a metaphysician who claimed to have knowledge of a reality which transcended the phenomenal world would be to enquire from what premises his propositions were deduced. Must he not begin, as other men do, with the evidence of his senses? And if so, what valid process of reasoning can possibly lead him to the conception of a transcendent reality? Surely from empirical premises nothing whatsoever concerning the properties, or even the existence, of anything super-empirical can legitimately be inferred. But this objection would be met by a denial on the part of the metaphysician that his assertions were ultimately based on the evidence of his senses. He would say that he was endowed with a faculty of intellectual intuition which enabled him to know facts that could not be known through sense-experience. And even if it could be shown that he was relying on empirical premises, and that his venture into a non-empirical world was therefore logically unjustified, it would not follow that the assertions which he made concerning this non-empirical world could not be true. For the fact that a conclusion does not follow from its putative premise is not sufficient to show that it is false. Consequently one cannot overthrow a system of transcendent metaphysics merely by criticising the way in which it comes into being. What is required is rather a criticism of the nature of the actual statements which comprise it. And this is the line of argument which we shall, in fact, pursue. For we shall maintain that no statement which refers to a "reality" transcending the limits of all possible sense-experience can possibly have any literal significance; from which it must follow that the labours of those who have striven to describe such a reality have all been devoted to the production of nonsense.

It may be suggested that this is a proposition which has already been proved by Kant. But although Kant also condemned transcendent metaphysics, he did so on different grounds. For he said that the human understanding was so constituted that it lost itself in contradictions when it ventured out beyond the limits of possible experience and attempted to deal with things in themselves. And thus he made the impossibility of a transcendent metaphysic not, as we do, a matter of logic, but a matter of fact. He asserted, not that our minds could not conceivably have had the power of penetrating beyond the phenomenal world, but merely that they were in fact devoid of it. And this leads the critic to ask how, if it is possible to know only what lies within the bounds of sense-experience, the author can be justified in asserting that real things do exist beyond, and how he can tell what are the boundaries beyond which the human understanding may not venture, unless he succeeds in passing them himself. As Wittgenstein says, "in order to draw a limit to thinking, we should have to think both sides of this limit,"[1] a truth to which Bradley gives a special twist in maintaining that the man who is ready to prove that metaphysics is impossible is a brother metaphysician with a rival theory of his own.[2]

[1] *Tractatus Logico-Philosophicus*, Preface.
[2] Bradley, *Appearance and Reality*, 2nd ed., p. 1.

Whatever force these objections may have against the Kantian doctrine, they have none whatsoever against the thesis that I am about to set forth. It cannot here be said that the author is himself overstepping the barrier he maintains to be impassable. For the fruitlessness of attempting to transcend the limits of possible sense-experience will be deduced, not from a psychological hypothesis concerning the actual constitution of the human mind, but from the rule which determines the literal significance of language. Our charge against the metaphysician is not that he attempts to employ the understanding in a field where it cannot profitably venture, but that he produces sentences which fail to conform to the conditions under which alone a sentence can be literally significant. Nor are we ourselves obliged to talk nonsense in order to show that all sentences of a certain type are necessarily devoid of literal significance. We need only formulate the criterion which enables us to test whether a sentence expresses a genuine proposition about a matter of fact, and then point out that the sentences under consideration fail to satisfy it. And this we shall now proceed to do. We shall first of all formulate the criterion in somewhat vague terms, and then give the explanations which are necessary to render it precise.

The criterion which we use to test the genuineness of apparent statements of fact is the criterion of verifiability. We say that a sentence is factually significant to any given person, if, and only if, he knows how to verify the proposition which it purports to express—that is, if he knows what observations would lead him, under certain conditions, to accept the proposition as being true, or reject it as being false. If, on the other hand, the putative proposition is of such a character that the assumption of its truth, or falsehood, is consistent with any assumption whatsoever concerning the nature of his future experience, then, as far as he is concerned, it is, if not a tautology, a mere pseudo-proposition. The sentence expressing it may be emotionally significant to him; but it is not literally significant. And with regard to questions the procedure is the same. We enquire in every case what observations would lead us to answer the question, one way or the other; and, if none can be discovered, we must conclude that the sentence under consideration does not, as far as we are concerned, express a genuine question, however strongly its grammatical appearance may suggest that it does.

As the adoption of this procedure is an essential factor in the argument of this book, it needs to be examined in detail.

In the first place, it is necessary to draw a distinction between practical verifiability, and verifiability in principle. Plainly we all understand, in many cases believe, propositions which we have not in fact taken steps to verify. Many of these are propositions which we could verify if we took enough trouble. But there remain a number of significant propositions, concerning matters of fact, which we could not verify even if we chose; simply because we lack the practical means of placing ourselves in the situation where the relevant observations could be made. A simple and familiar example of such a proposition is the proposition that there are mountains on the farther side of the moon.[1] No rocket has yet been invented which would enable me to go and look at the farther side of the moon, so that I am unable to decide the matter by actual observation. But I do know what observations would decide it for me, if, as is theoretically conceivable, I were once in a position to make them. And therefore I say that the proposition is verifiable in principle, if not in practice, and is accordingly significant. On the other hand, such a metaphysical pseudo-proposition as "the Absolute enters into, but is itself incapable of, evolution and progress,"[2] is not even in principle verifiable. For one cannot conceive of an observation which would enable one to determine whether the Absolute did, or did not, enter into evolution and progress. Of course it is possible that the author of such a remark is using English words in a way in which they are not commonly used by English-speaking people, and that he does, in fact, intend to assert something which could be empirically verified. But until he makes us understand how the proposition that he wishes to express would be verified, he fails to communicate anything to us. And if he admits, as I think the author of the remark in question would have admitted, that his words were not intended to express either a tautology or a proposition which was capable, at least in principle, of being verified, then it follows that he has made an utterance which has no literal significance even for himself.

A further distinction which we must make is the distinction

[1] This example has been used by Professor Schlick to illustrate the same point.

[2] A remark taken at random from *Appearance and Reality*, by F. H. Bradley.

between the "strong" and the "weak" sense of the term "verifiable." A proposition is said to be verifiable, in the strong sense of the term, if, and only if, its truth could be conclusively established in experience. But it is verifiable, in the weak sense, if it is possible for experience to render it probable. In which sense are we using the term when we say that a putative proposition is genuine only if it is verifiable?

It seems to me that if we adopt conclusive verifiability as our criterion of significance, as some positivists have proposed,[1] our argument will prove too much. Consider, for example, the case of general propositions of law—such propositions, namely, as "arsenic is poisonous"; "all men are mortal"; "a body tends to expand when it is heated." It is of the very nature of these propositions that their truth cannot be established with certainty by any finite series of observations. But if it is recognised that such general propositions of law are designed to cover an infinite number of cases, then it must be admitted that they cannot, even in principle, be verified conclusively. And then, if we adopt conclusive verifiability as our criterion of significance, we are logically obliged to treat these general propositions of law in the same fashion as we treat the statements of the metaphysician.

In face of this difficulty, some positivists[2] have adopted the heroic course of saying that these general propositions are indeed pieces of nonsense, albeit an essentially important type of nonsense. But here the introduction of the term "important" is simply an attempt to hedge. It serves only to mark the authors' recognition that their view is somewhat too paradoxical, without in any way removing the paradox. Besides, the difficulty is not confined to the case of general propositions of law, though it is there revealed most plainly. It is hardly less obvious in the case of propositions about the remote past. For it must surely be admitted that, however strong the evidence in favour of historical statements may be, their truth can never become more than highly probable. And to maintain that they also constituted an important, or unimportant, type of nonsense would be unplausible, to say the very least. Indeed, it will be our contention

---

[1] e.g. M. Schlick, "Positivismus und Realismus," *Erkenntnis*, Vol. I, 1930. F. Waismann, "Logische Analyse des Warscheinlichkeitsbegriffs," *Erkenntnis*, Vol. I, 1930.

[2] e.g. M. Schlick, "Die Kausalität in der gegenwärtigen Physik," *Naturwissenschaft*, Vol. 19, 1931.

that no proposition, other than a tautology, can possibly be anything more than a probable hypothesis. And if this is correct, the principle that a sentence can be factually significant only if it expresses what is conclusively verifiable is self-stultifying as a criterion of significance. For it leads to the conclusion that it is impossible to make a significant statement of fact at all.

Nor can we accept the suggestion that a sentence should be allowed to be factually significant if, and only if, it expresses something which is definitely confutable by experience.[1] Those who adopt this course assume that, although no finite series of observations is ever sufficient to establish the truth of a hypothesis beyond all possibility of doubt, there are crucial cases in which a single observation, or series of observations, can definitely confute it. But, as we shall show later on, this assumption is false. A hypothesis cannot be conclusively confuted any more than it can be conclusively verified. For when we take the occurrence of certain observations as proof that a given hypothesis is false, we presuppose the existence of certain conditions. And though, in any given case, it may be extremely improbable that this assumption is false, it is not logically impossible. We shall see that there need be no self-contradiction in holding that some of the relevant circumstances are other than we have taken them to be, and consequently that the hypothesis has not really broken down. And if it is not the case that any hypothesis can be definitely confuted, we cannot hold that the genuineness of a proposition depends on the possibility of its definite confutation.

Accordingly, we fall back on the weaker sense of verification. We say that the question that must be asked about any putative statement of fact is not, Would any observations make its truth or falsehood logically certain? but simply, Would any observations be relevant to the determination of its truth or falsehood? And it is only if a negative answer is given to this second question that we conclude that the statement under consideration is nonsensical.

To make our position clearer, we may formulate it in another way. Let us call a proposition which records an actual or possible observation an experiential proposition. Then we may say that it is the mark of a genuine factual proposition, not that it should be equivalent to an experiential proposition, or any finite number

---
[1] This has been proposed by Karl Popper in his *Logik der Forschung*.

of experiential propositions, but simply that some experiential propositions can be deduced from it in conjunction with certain other premises without being deducible from those other premises alone.[1]

This criterion seems liberal enough. In contrast to the principle of conclusive verifiability, it clearly does not deny significance to general propositions, or to propositions about the past. Let us see what kinds of assertion it rules out.

A good example of the kind of utterance that is condemned by our criterion as being not even false but nonsensical would be the assertion that the world of sense-experience was altogether unreal. It must, of course, be admitted that our senses do sometimes deceive us. We may, as the result of having certain sensations, expect certain other sensations to be obtainable which are, in fact, not obtainable. But, in all such cases, it is further sense-experience that informs us of the mistakes that arise out of sense-experience. We say that the senses sometimes deceive us, just because the expectations to which our sense-experiences give rise do not always accord with what we subsequently experience. That is, we rely on our senses to substantiate or confute the judgements which are based on our sensations. And therefore the fact that our perceptual judgements are sometimes found to be erroneous has not the slightest tendency to show that the world of sense-experience is unreal. And, indeed, it is plain that no conceivable observation, or series of observations, could have any tendency to show that the world revealed to us by sense-experience was unreal. Consequently, anyone who condemns the sensible world as a world of mere appearance, as opposed to reality, is saying something which, according to our criterion of significance, is literally nonsensical.

An example of a controversy which the application of our criterion obliges us to condemn as fictitious is provided by those who dispute concerning the number of substances that there are in the world. For it is admitted both by monists, who maintain that reality is one substance, and by pluralists, who maintain that reality is many, that it is impossible to imagine any empirical situation which would be relevant to the solution of their dispute. But if we are told that no possible observation could give any

<hr/>

[1] This is an over-simplified statement, which is not literally correct. I give what I believe to be the correct formulation in the Introduction, p. 13.

39

probability either to the assertion that reality was one substance or to the assertion that it was many, then we must conclude that neither assertion is significant. We shall see later on[1] that there are genuine logical and empirical questions involved in the dispute between monists and pluralists. But the metaphysical question concerning "substance" is ruled out by our criterion as spurious.

A similar treatment must be accorded to the controversy between realists and idealists, in its metaphysical aspect. A simple illustration, which I have made use of in a similar argument elsewhere,[2] will help to demonstrate this. Let us suppose that a picture is discovered and the suggestion made that it was painted by Goya. There is a definite procedure for dealing with such a question. The experts examine the picture to see in what way it resembles the accredited works of Goya, and to see if it bears any marks which are characteristic of a forgery; they look up contemporary records for evidence of the existence of such a picture, and so on. In the end, they may still disagree, but each one knows what empirical evidence would go to confirm or discredit his opinion. Suppose, now, that these men have studied philosophy, and some of them proceed to maintain that this picture is a set of ideas in the perceiver's mind, or in God's mind, others that it is objectively real. What possible experience could any of them have which would be relevant to the solution of this dispute one way or the other? In the ordinary sense of the term "real," in which it is opposed to "illusory," the reality of the picture is not in doubt. The disputants have satisfied themselves that the picture is real, in this sense, by obtaining a correlated series of sensations of sight and sensations of touch. Is there any similar process by which they could discover whether the picture was real, in the sense in which the term "real" is opposed to "ideal"? Clearly there is none. But, if that is so, the problem is fictitious according to our criterion. This does not mean that the realist-idealist controversy may be dismissed without further ado. For it can legitimately be regarded as a dispute concerning the analysis of existential propositions, and so as involving a logical problem which, as we shall see, can be definitively solved.[3] What we have just shown is that the question at issue between idealists and

[1] In Chapter VIII.
[2] Vide "Demonstration of the Impossibility of Metaphysics," *Mind*, 1934, p. 339.
[3] Vide Chapter VIII.

40

realists becomes fictitious when, as is often the case, it is given a metaphysical interpretation.

There is no need for us to give further examples of the operation of our criterion of significance. For our object is merely to show that philosophy, as a genuine branch of knowledge, must be distinguished from metaphysics. We are not now concerned with the historical question how much of what has traditionally passed for philosophy is actually metaphysical. We shall, however, point out later on that the majority of the "great philosophers" of the past were not essentially metaphysicians, and thus reassure those who would otherwise be prevented from adopting our criterion by considerations of piety.

As to the validity of the verification principle, in the form in which we have stated it, a demonstration will be given in the course of this book. For it will be shown that all propositions which have factual content are empirical hypotheses; and that the function of an empirical hypothesis is to provide a rule for the anticipation of experience.[1] And this means that every empirical hypothesis must be relevant to some actual, or possible, experience, so that a statement which is not relevant to any experience is not an empirical hypothesis, and accordingly has no factual content. But this is precisely what the principle of verifiability asserts.

It should be mentioned here that the fact that the utterances of the metaphysician are nonsensical does not follow simply from the fact that they are devoid of factual content. It follows from that fact, together with the fact that they are not *a priori* propositions. And in assuming that they are not *a priori* propositions, we are once again anticipating the conclusions of a later chapter in this book.[2] For it will be shown there that *a priori* propositions, which have always been attractive to philosophers on account of their certainty, owe this certainty to the fact that they are tautologies. We may accordingly define a metaphysical sentence as a sentence which purports to express a genuine proposition, but does, in fact, express neither a tautology nor an empirical hypothesis. And as tautologies and empirical hypotheses form the entire class of significant propositions, we are justified in concluding that all metaphysical assertions are nonsensical. Our next task is to show how they come to be made.

[1] Vide Chapter V. [2] Chapter IV.

The use of the term "substance," to which we have already referred, provides us with a good example of the way in which metaphysics mostly comes to be written. It happens to be the case that we cannot, in our language, refer to the sensible properties of a thing without introducing a word or phrase which appears to stand for the thing itself as opposed to anything which may be said about it. And, as a result of this, those who are infected by the primitive superstition that to every name a single real entity must correspond assume that it is necessary to distinguish logically between the thing itself and any, or all, of its sensible properties. And so they employ the term "substance" to refer to the thing itself. But from the fact that we happen to employ a single word to refer to a thing, and make that word the grammatical subject of the sentences in which we refer to the sensible appearances of the thing, it does not by any means follow that the thing itself is a "simple entity," or that it cannot be defined in terms of the totality of its appearances. It is true that in talking of "its" appearances we appear to distinguish the thing from the appearances, but that is simply an accident of linguistic usage. Logical analysis shows that what makes these "appearances" the "appearances of" the same thing is not their relationship to an entity other than themselves, but their relationship to one another. The metaphysician fails to see this because he is misled by a superficial grammatical feature of his language.

A simpler and clearer instance of the way in which a consideration of grammar leads to metaphysics is the case of the metaphysical concept of Being. The origin of our temptation to raise questions about Being, which no conceivable experience would enable us to answer, lies in the fact that, in our language, sentences which express existential propositions and sentences which express attributive propositions may be of the same grammatical form. For instance, the sentences "Martyrs exist" and "Martyrs suffer" both consist of a noun followed by an intransitive verb, and the fact that they have grammatically the same appearance leads one to assume that they are of the same logical type. It is seen that in the proposition "Martyrs suffer," the members of a certain species are credited with a certain attribute, and it is sometimes assumed that the same thing is true of such a proposition as "Martyrs exist." If this were actually the case, it would, indeed, be as legitimate to speculate about the Being of martyrs as it is to speculate about their suffering. But, as Kant pointed out,[1] existence is not an attribute. For, when we ascribe an attribute to a thing, we covertly assert that it exists: so that if existence were itself an attribute, it would follow that all positive existential propositions were tautologies, and all negative existential propositions self-contradictory; and this is not the case.[2] So that those who raise questions about Being which are based on the assumption that existence is an attribute are guilty of following grammar beyond the boundaries of sense.

A similar mistake has been made in connection with such propositions as "Unicorns are fictitious." Here again the fact that there is a superficial grammatical resemblance between the English sentences "Dogs are faithful" and "Unicorns are fictitious," and between the corresponding sentences in other languages, creates the assumption that they are of the same logical type. Dogs must exist in order to have the property of being faithful, and so it is held that unless unicorns in some way existed they could not have the property of being fictitious. But, as it is plainly self-contradictory to say that fictitious objects exist, the device is adopted of saying that they are real in some non-empirical sense—that they have a mode of real being which is different from the mode of being of existent things. But since there is no way of testing whether an object is real in this sense, as there is for testing whether it is real in the ordinary sense, the assertion that fictitious objects have a special non-empirical mode of real being is devoid of all literal significance. It comes to be made as a result of the assumption that being fictitious is an attribute. And this is a fallacy of the same order as the fallacy of supposing that existence is an attribute, and it can be exposed in the same way.

In general, the postulation of real non-existent entities results from the superstition, just now referred to, that, to every word or phrase that can be the grammatical subject of a sentence, there must somewhere be a real entity corresponding. For as there is no place in the empirical world for many of these "entities," a special non-empirical world is invoked to house them. To this error must be attributed, not only the utterances of a Heidegger,

[1] Vide *The Critique of Pure Reason*, "Transcendental Dialectic," Book II, Chapter iii, section 4.

[2] This argument is well stated by John Wisdom, *Interpretation and Analysis*, pp. 62, 63.

43

who bases his metaphysics on the assumption that "Nothing" is a name which is used to denote something peculiarly mysterious,[1] but also the prevalence of such problems as those concerning the reality of propositions and universals whose senselessness, though less obvious, is no less complete.

These few examples afford a sufficient indication of the way in which most metaphysical assertions come to be formulated. They show how easy it is to write sentences which are literally nonsensical without seeing that they are nonsensical. And thus we see that the view that a number of the traditional "problems of philosophy" are metaphysical, and consequently fictitious, does not involve any incredible assumptions about the psychology of philosophers.

Among those who recognise that if philosophy is to be accounted a genuine branch of knowledge it must be defined in such a way as to distinguish it from metaphysics, it is fashionable to speak of the metaphysician as a kind of misplaced poet. As his statements have no literal meaning, they are not subject to any criteria of truth or falsehood: but they may still serve to express, or arouse, emotion, and thus be subject to ethical or æsthetic standards. And it is suggested that they may have considerable value, as means of moral inspiration, or even as works of art. In this way, an attempt is made to compensate the metaphysician for his extrusion from philosophy.[2]

I am afraid that this compensation is hardly in accordance with his deserts. The view that the metaphysician is to be reckoned among the poets appears to rest on the assumption that both talk nonsense. But this assumption is false. In the vast majority of cases the sentences which are produced by poets do have literal meaning. The difference between the man who uses language scientifically and the man who uses it emotively is not that the one produces sentences which are incapable of arousing emotion, and the other sentences which have no sense, but that the one is primarily concerned with the expression of true propositions, the other with the creation of a work of art. Thus, if a work of science

---

[1] Vide *Was ist Metaphysik*, by Heidegger: criticised by Rudolf Carnap in his "Überwindung der Metaphysik durch logische Analyse der Sprache," *Erkenntnis*, Vol. II, 1932.

[2] For a discussion of this point, see also C. A. Mace, "Representation and Expression," *Analysis*, Vol. I, No. 3; and "Metaphysics and Emotive Language," *Analysis*, Vol. II, Nos. 1 and 2.

contains true and important propositions, its value as a work of science will hardly be diminished by the fact that they are inelegantly expressed. And similarly, a work of art is not necessarily the worse for the fact that all the propositions comprising it are literally false. But to say that many literary works are largely composed of falsehoods, is not to say that they are composed of pseudo-propositions. It is, in fact, very rare for a literary artist to produce sentences which have no literal meaning. And where this does occur, the sentences are carefully chosen for their rhythm and balance. If the author writes nonsense, it is because he considers it most suitable for bringing about the effects for which his writing is designed.

The metaphysician, on the other hand, does not intend to write nonsense. He lapses into it through being deceived by grammar, or through committing errors of reasoning, such as that which leads to the view that the sensible world is unreal. But it is not the mark of a poet simply to make mistakes of this sort. There are some, indeed, who would see in the fact that the metaphysician's utterances are senseless a reason against the view that they have æsthetic value. And, without going so far as this, we may safely say that it does not constitute a reason for it.

It is true, however, that although the greater part of metaphysics is merely the embodiment of humdrum errors, there remain a number of metaphysical passages which are the work of genuine mystical feeling; and they may more plausibly be held to have moral or æsthetic value. But, as far as we are concerned, the distinction between the kind of metaphysics that is produced by a philosopher who has been duped by grammar, and the kind that is produced by a mystic who is trying to express the inexpressible, is of no great importance: what is important to us is to realise that even the utterances of the metaphysician who is attempting to expound a vision are literally senseless; so that henceforth we may pursue our philosophical researches with as little regard for them as for the more inglorious kind of metaphysics which comes from a failure to understand the workings of our language.

CHAPTER II

THE FUNCTION OF PHILOSOPHY

Among the superstitions from which we are freed by the abandonment of metaphysics is the view that it is the business of the philosopher to construct a deductive system. In rejecting this view we are not, of course, suggesting that the philosopher can dispense with deductive reasoning. We are simply contesting his right to posit certain first principles, and then offer them with their consequences as a complete picture of reality. To discredit this procedure, one has only to show that there can be no first principles of the kind it requires.

As it is the function of these first principles to provide a certain basis for our knowledge, it is clear that they are not to be found among the so-called laws of nature. For we shall see that the "laws of nature," if they are not mere definitions, are simply hypotheses which may be confuted by experience. And, indeed, it has never been the practice of the system-builders in philosophy to choose inductive generalizations for their premises. Rightly regarding such generalizations as being merely probable, they subordinate them to principles which they believe to be logically certain.

This is illustrated most clearly in the system of Descartes. It is commonly said that Descartes attempted to derive all human knowledge from premises whose truth was intuitively certain: but this interpretation puts an undue stress on the element of psychology in his system. I think he realised well enough that a mere appeal to intuition was insufficient for his purpose, since men are not all equally credulous, and that what he was really trying to do was to base all our knowledge on propositions which it would be self-contradictory to deny. He thought he had found such a proposition in *"cogito,"* which must not here be understood in its ordinary sense of "I think," but rather as meaning "there is a thought now." In fact he was wrong, because *"non cogito"* would be self-contradictory only if it negated itself: and this no significant proposition can do. But even if it were true that such a proposition as "there is a thought now" was logically certain, it still would not serve Descartes' purpose. For if *"cogito"* is taken in this sense, his initial principle, *"cogito ergo sum,"* is false. "I exist" does not follow from "there is a thought now." The fact that a thought occurs at a given moment does not entail that any other thought has occurred at any other moment, still less that there has occurred a series of thoughts sufficient to constitute a single self. As Hume conclusively showed, no one event intrinsically points to any other. We infer the existence of events which we are not actually observing, with the help of general principles. But these principles must be obtained inductively. By mere deduction from what is immediately given we cannot advance a single step beyond. And, consequently, any attempt to base a deductive system on propositions which describe what is immediately given is bound to be a failure.

The only other course open to one who wished to deduce all our knowledge from "first principles," without indulging in metaphysics, would be to take for his premises a set of *a priori* truths. But, as we have already mentioned, and shall later show, an *a priori* truth is a tautology. And from a set of tautologies, taken by themselves, only further tautologies can be validly deduced. But it would be absurd to put forward a system of tautologies as constituting the whole truth about the universe. And thus we may conclude that it is not possible to deduce all our knowledge from "first principles"; so that those who hold that it is the function of philosophy to carry out such a deduction are denying its claim to be a genuine branch of knowledge.

The belief that it is the business of the philosopher to search for first principles is bound up with the familiar conception of philosophy as the study of reality as a whole. And this conception is one which it is difficult to criticize, because it is so vague. If it is taken to imply, as it sometimes is, that the philosopher somehow projects himself outside the world, and takes a bird's-eye view of it, then it is plainly a metaphysical conception. And it is also metaphysical to assert, as some do, that "reality as a whole" is somehow generically different from the reality which is investigated piecemeal by the special sciences. But if the assertion that philosophy studies reality as a whole is understood to imply merely that the philosopher is equally concerned with the content of every science, then we may accept it, not indeed as an adequate definition of philosophy, but as a truth about it. For we shall find, when we come to discuss the relationship of philosophy to science, that it is not, in principle, related to any one science more closely than to any other.

In saying that philosophy is concerned with each of the sciences, in a manner which we shall indicate,[1] we mean also to rule out the supposition that philosophy can be ranged alongside the existing sciences, as a special department of speculative knowledge. Those who make this supposition cherish the belief that there are some things in the world which are possible objects of speculative knowledge and yet lie beyond the scope of empirical science. But this belief is a delusion. There is no field of experience which cannot, in principle, be brought under some form of scientific law, and no type of speculative knowledge about the world which it is, in principle, beyond the power of science to give. We have already gone some way to substantiate this proposition by demolishing metaphysics; and we shall justify it to the full in the course of this book.

With this we complete the overthrow of speculative philosophy. We are now in a position to see that the function of philosophy is wholly critical. In what exactly does its critical activity consist?

One way of answering this question is to say that it is the philosopher's business to test the validity of our scientific hypotheses and everyday assumptions. But this view, though very widely held, is mistaken. If a man chooses to doubt the truth of all the propositions he ordinarily believes, it is not in the power of philosophy to reassure him. The most that philosophy can do, apart from seeing whether his beliefs are self-consistent, is to show what are the criteria which are used to determine the truth or falsehood of any given proposition: and then, when the sceptic realises that certain observations would verify his propositions, he may also realize that he could make those observations, and so consider his original beliefs to be justified. But in such a case one cannot say that it is philosophy which justifies his beliefs. Philosophy merely shows him that experience can justify them. We may look to the philosopher to show us what we accept as constituting sufficient evidence for the truth of any given

[1] Vide Chapter III and Chapter VIII.

empirical proposition. But whether the evidence is forthcoming or not is in every case a purely empirical question.

If anyone thinks that we are here taking too much for granted, let him refer to the chapter on "Truth and Probability," in which we discuss how the validity of synthetic propositions is determined. He will see there that the only sort of justification that is necessary or possible for self-consistent empirical propositions is empirical verification. And this applies just as much to the laws of science as to the maxims of common sense. Indeed there is no difference in kind between them. The superiority of the scientific hypothesis consists merely in its being more abstract, more precise, and more fruitful. And although scientific objects such as atoms and electrons seem to be fictitious in a way that chairs and tables are not, here, too, the distinction is only a distinction of degree. For both these kinds of objects are known only by their sensible manifestations and are definable in terms of them.

It is time, therefore, to abandon the superstition that natural science cannot be regarded as logically respectable until philosophers have solved the problem of induction. The problem of induction is, roughly speaking, the problem of finding a way to prove that certain empirical generalizations which are derived from past experience will hold good also in the future. There are only two ways of approaching this problem on the assumption that it is a genuine problem, and it is easy to see that neither of them can lead to its solution. One may attempt to deduce the proposition which one is required to prove either from a purely formal principle or from an empirical principle. In the former case one commits the error of supposing that from a tautology it is possible to deduce a proposition about a matter of fact; in the latter case one simply assumes what one is setting out to prove. For example, it is often said that we can justify induction by invoking the uniformity of nature, or by postulating a "principle of limited independent variety."[1] But, in fact, the principle of the uniformity of nature merely states, in a misleading fashion, the assumption that past experience is a reliable guide to the future; while the principle of limited independent variety presupposes it. And it is plain that any other empirical principle which was put forward as a justification of induction would beg the question in the same way. For the only grounds which one

[1] cf. J. M. Keynes, *A Treatise on Probability*, Part III.

could have for believing such a principle would be inductive grounds.

Thus it appears that there is no possible way of solving the problem of induction, as it is ordinarily conceived. And this means that it is a fictitious problem, since all genuine problems are at least theoretically capable of being solved: and the credit of natural science is not impaired by the fact that some philosophers continue to be puzzled by it. Actually, we shall see that the only test to which a form of scientific procedure which satisfies the necessary condition of self-consistency is subject, is the test of its success in practice. We are entitled to have faith in our procedure just so long as it does the work which it is designed to do— that is, enables us to predict future experience, and so to control our environment. Of course, the fact that a certain form of procedure has always been successful in practice affords no logical guarantee that it will continue to be so. But then it is a mistake to demand a guarantee where it is logically impossible to obtain one. This does not mean that it is irrational to expect future experience to conform to the past. For when we come to define "rationality" we shall find that for us "being rational" entails being guided in a particular fashion by past experience.

The task of defining rationality is precisely the sort of task that it is the business of philosophy to undertake. But in achieving this it does not justify scientific procedure. What justifies scientific procedure, to the extent to which it is capable of being justified, is the success of the predictions to which it gives rise: and this can be determined only in actual experience. By itself, the analysis of a synthetic principle tells us nothing whatsoever about its truth.

Unhappily, this fact is generally disregarded by philosophers who concern themselves with the so-called theory of knowledge. Thus it is common for writers on the subject of perception to assume that, unless one can give a satisfactory analysis of perceptual situations, one is not entitled to believe in the existence of material things. But this is a complete mistake. What gives one the right to believe in the existence of a certain material thing is simply the fact that one has certain sensations: for, whether one realises it or not, to say that the thing exists is equivalent to saying that such sensations are obtainable. It is the philosopher's business to give a correct definition of material things in terms of sensations. But his success or failure in this task has no bearing whatsoever on the validity of our perceptual judgements. That depends wholly on actual sense-experience.

It follows that the philosopher has no right to despise the beliefs of common sense. If he does so, he merely displays his ignorance of the true purpose of his enquiries. What he is entitled to despise is the unreflecting analysis of those beliefs, which takes the grammatical structure of the sentence as a trustworthy guide to its meaning. Thus, many of the mistakes made in connection with the problem of perception can be accounted for by the fact, already referred to in connection with the metaphysical notion of "substance," that it happens to be impossible in an ordinary European language to mention a thing without appearing to distinguish it generically from its qualities and states. But from the fact that the common-sense analysis of a proposition is mistaken it by no means follows that the proposition is not true. The philosopher may be able to show us that the propositions we believe are far more complex than we suppose; but it does not follow from this that we have no right to believe them.

It should now be sufficiently clear that if the philosopher is to uphold his claim to make a special contribution to the stock of our knowledge, he must not attempt to formulate speculative truths, or to look for first principles, or to make *a priori* judgements about the validity of our empirical beliefs. He must, in fact, confine himself to works of clarification and analysis of a sort which we shall presently describe.

In saying that the activity of philosophising is essentially analytic, we are not, of course, maintaining that all those who are commonly called philosophers have actually been engaged in carrying out analyses. On the contrary, we have been at pains to show that a great deal of what is commonly called philosophy is metaphysical in character. What we have been in search of, in enquiring into the function of philosophy, is a definition of philosophy which should accord to some extent with the practice of those who are commonly called philosophers, and at the same time be consistent with the common assumption that philosophy is a special branch of knowledge. It is because metaphysics fails to satisfy this second condition that we distinguish it from philosophy, in spite of the fact that it is commonly referred to as philosophy. And our justification for making this distinction is that it is necessitated by our original postulate that philosophy is a special branch of knowledge, and our demonstration that metaphysics is not.

Although this procedure is logically unassailable, it will perhaps be attacked on the ground that it is inexpedient. It will be said that the "history of philosophy" is, almost entirely, a history of metaphysics; and, consequently, that although there is no actual fallacy involved in our using the word "philosophy" in the sense in which philosophy is incompatible with metaphysics, it is dangerously misleading. For all our care in defining the term will not prevent people from confusing the activities which we call philosophical with the metaphysical activities of those whom they have been taught to regard as philosophers. And therefore it would surely be advisable for us to abandon the term "philosophy" altogether, as a name for a distinctive branch of knowledge, and invent some new description for the activity which we were minded to call the activity of philosophizing.

Our answer to this is that it is not the case that the "history of philosophy" is almost entirely a history of metaphysics. That it contains some metaphysics is undeniable. But I think it can be shown that the majority of those who are commonly supposed to have been great philosophers were primarily not metaphysicians but analysts. For example, I do not see how anyone who follows the account which we shall give of the nature of philosophical analysis and then turns to Locke's *Essay Concerning Human Understanding* can fail to conclude that it is essentially an analytic work. Locke is generally regarded as being one who, like G. E. Moore at the present time, puts forward a philosophy of common sense.[1] But he does not, any more than Moore, attempt to give an *a priori* justification of our common-sense beliefs. Rather does he appear to have seen that it was not his business as a philosopher to affirm or deny the validity of any empirical propositions, but only to analyse them. For he is content, in his own words, "to be employed as an under-labourer in clearing the ground a little, and removing some of the rubbish that lies in the way of knowledge"; and so devotes himself to the purely analytic tasks of defining knowledge, and classifying propositions, and displaying the nature of material things. And the small portion of his work

[1] Vide G. E. Moore, "A Defence of Common Sense," *Contemporary British Philosophy*, Vol. II.

which is not philosophical, in our sense, is not given over to metaphysics, but to psychology.

Nor is it fair to regard Berkeley as a metaphysician. For he did not, in fact, deny the reality of material things, as we are still too commonly told. What he denied was the adequacy of Locke's analysis of the notion of a material thing. He maintained that to say of various "ideas of sensation" that they belonged to a single material thing was not, as Locke thought, to say that they were related to a single unobservable underlying "somewhat," but rather that they stood in certain relations to one another. And in this he was right. Admittedly he made the mistake of supposing that what was immediately given in sensation was necessarily mental; and the use, by him and by Locke, of the word "idea" to denote an element in that which is sensibly given is objectionable, because it suggests this false view. Accordingly we replace the word "idea" in this usage by the neutral word "sense-content," which we shall use to refer to the immediate data not merely of "outer" but also of "introspective" sensation, and say that what Berkeley discovered was that material things must be definable in terms of sense-contents. We shall see, when we come finally to settle the conflict between idealism and realism, that his actual conception of the relationship between material things and sense-contents was not altogether accurate. It led him to some notoriously paradoxical conclusions, which a slight emendation will enable us to avoid. But the fact that he failed to give a completely correct account of the way in which material things are constituted out of sense-contents does not invalidate his contention that they are so constituted. On the contrary, we know that it must be possible to define material things in terms of sense-contents, because it is only by the occurrence of certain sense-contents that the existence of any material thing can ever be in the least degree verified. And thus we see that we have not to enquire whether a phenomenalist "theory of perception" or some other sort of theory is correct, but only what form of phenomenalist theory is correct. For the fact that all causal and representative theories of perception treat material things as if they were unobservable entities entitles us, as Berkeley saw, to rule them out *a priori*. The unfortunate thing is that, in spite of this, he found it necessary to postulate God as an unobservable cause of our "ideas"; and he must be criticised also for failing to see that the argument which he uses to dispose of Locke's analysis of a material thing is fatal to his own conception of the nature of the self, a point which was effectively seized upon by Hume.

Of Hume we may say not merely that he was not in practice a metaphysician, but that he explicitly rejected metaphysics. We find the strongest evidence of this in the passage with which he concludes his *Enquiry Concerning Human Understanding.* "If," he says, "we take in our hand any volume; of divinity, or school metaphysics, for instance; let us ask, Does it contain any abstract reasoning concerning quantity or number? No. Does it contain any experimental reasoning concerning matter of fact and existence? No. Commit it then to the flames. For it can contain nothing but sophistry and illusion." What is this but a rhetorical version of our own thesis that a sentence which does not express either a formally true proposition or an empirical hypothesis is devoid of literal significance? It is true that Hume does not, so far as I know, actually put forward any view concerning the nature of philosophical propositions themselves, but those of his works which are commonly accounted philosophical are, apart from certain passages which deal with questions of psychology, works of analysis. If this is not universally conceded, it is because his treatment of causation, which is the main feature of his philosophical work, is often misinterpreted. He has been accused of denying causation, whereas in fact he was concerned only with defining it. So far is he from asserting that no causal propositions are true that he is himself at pains to give rules for judging of the existence of causes and effects.[1] He realised well enough that the question whether a given causal proposition was true or false was not one that could be settled *a priori*, and accordingly confined himself to discussing the analytic question, What is it that we are asserting when we assert that one event is causally connected with another? And in answering this question he showed, I think conclusively, first that the relation of cause and effect was not logical in character, since any proposition asserting a causal connection could be denied without self-contradiction, secondly that causal laws were not analytically derived from experience, since they were not deducible from any finite number of experiential propositions, and, thirdly, that it was a mistake to analyse propositions asserting causal connections in terms of a relation of

[1] Vide *A Treatise of Human Nature*, Book I, Part III, section 15.

necessitation which held between particular events, since it was impossible to conceive of any observations which would have the slightest tendency to establish the existence of such a relation. He thus laid the way open for the view, which we adopt, that every assertion of a particular causal connection involves the assertion of a causal law, and that every general proposition of the form "C causes E" is equivalent to a proposition of the form "whenever C, then E," where the symbol "whenever" must be taken to refer, not to a finite number of actual instances of C, but to the infinite number of possible instances. He himself defines a cause as "an object, followed by another, and where all the objects similar to the first are followed by objects similar to the second," or, alternatively, as "an object followed by another, and whose appearance always conveys the thought to that other";[1] but neither of these definitions is acceptable as it stands. For, even if it is true that we should not, according to our standards of rationality, have good reason to believe that an event C was the cause of an event E unless we had observed a constant conjunction of events like C with events like E, still there is no self-contradiction involved in asserting the proposition "C is the cause of E" and at the same time denying that any events like C or like E ever have been observed; and this would be self-contradictory if the first of the definitions quoted was correct. Nor is it inconceivable, as the second definition implies, that there should be causal laws which have never yet been thought of. But although we are obliged, for these reasons, to reject Hume's actual definitions of a cause, our view of the nature of causation remains substantially the same as his. And we agree with him that there can be no other justification for inductive reasoning than its success in practice, while insisting more strongly than he did that no better justification is required. For it is his failure to make this second point clear that has given his views the air of paradox which has caused them to be so much undervalued and misunderstood.

When we consider, also, that Hobbes and Bentham were chiefly occupied in giving definitions, and that the best part of John Stuart Mill's work consists in a development of the analyses carried out by Hume, we may fairly claim that in holding that the activity of philosophising is essentially analytic we are

[1] *An Enquiry Concerning Human Understanding*, section 7.

adopting a standpoint which has always been implicit in English empiricism. Not that the practice of philosophical analysis has been confined to members of this school. But it is with them that we have the closest historical affinity.

If I refrain from discussing these questions in detail, and make no attempt to furnish a complete list of all the "great philosophers" whose work is predominantly analytic—a list which would certainly include Plato and Aristotle and Kant—it is because the point to which this discussion is relevant is one of minor importance in our enquiry. We have been maintaining that much of "traditional philosophy" is genuinely philosophical, by our standards, in order to defend ourselves against the charge that our retention of the word "philosophy" is misleading. But even if it were the case that none of those who are commonly called philosophers had ever been engaged in what we call the activity of philosophising, it would not follow that our definition of philosophy was erroneous, given our initial postulates. We may admit that our retention of the word "philosophy" is causally dependent on our belief in the historical propositions set forth above. But the validity of these historical propositions has no logical bearing on the validity of our definition of philosophy, nor on the validity of the distinction between philosophy, in our sense, and metaphysics.

It is advisable to stress the point that philosophy, as we understand it, is wholly independent of metaphysics, inasmuch as the analytic method is commonly supposed by its critics to have a metaphysical basis. Being misled by the associations of the word "analysis," they assume that philosophical analysis is an activity of dissection; that it consists in "breaking up" objects into their constituent parts, until the whole universe is ultimately exhibited as an aggregate of "bare particulars," united by external relations. If this were really so, the most effective way of attacking the method would be to show that its basic presupposition was nonsensical. For to say that the universe was an aggregate of bare particulars would be as senseless as to say that it was Fire or Water or Experience. It is plain that no possible observation would enable one to verify such an assertion. But, so far as I know, this line of criticism is in fact never adopted. The critics content themselves with pointing out that few, if any, of the complex objects in the world are simply the sum of their parts.

They have a structure, an organic unity, which distinguishes them, as genuine wholes, from mere aggregates. But the analyst, so it is said, is obliged by his atomistic metaphysics to regard an object consisting of parts a, b, c, and d in a distinctive configuration as being simply $a+b+c+d$, and thus gives an entirely false account of its nature.

If we follow the Gestalt psychologists, who of all men talk most constantly about genuine wholes, in defining such a whole as one in which the properties of every part depend to some extent on its position in the whole, then we may accept it as an empirical fact that there exist genuine, or organic, wholes. And if the analytic method involved a denial of this fact, it would indeed be a faulty method. But, actually, the validity of the analytic method is not dependent on any empirical, much less any metaphysical, presupposition about the nature of things. For the philosopher, as an analyst, is not directly concerned with the physical properties of things. He is concerned only with the way in which we speak about them.

In other words, the propositions of philosophy are not factual, but linguistic in character—that is, they do not describe the behaviour of physical, or even mental, objects; they express definitions, or the formal consequences of definitions. Accordingly, we may say that philosophy is a department of logic. For we shall see that the characteristic mark of a purely logical enquiry is that it is concerned with the formal consequences of our definitions and not with questions of empirical fact.

It follows that philosophy does not in any way compete with science. The difference in type between philosophical and scientific propositions is such that they cannot conceivably contradict one another. And this makes it clear that the possibility of philosophical analysis is independent of any empirical assumptions. That it is independent of any metaphysical assumptions should be even more obvious still. For it is absurd to suppose that the provision of definitions, and the study of their formal consequences, involves the nonsensical assertion that the world is composed of bare particulars, or any other metaphysical dogma.

What has contributed as much as anything to the prevalent misunderstanding of the nature of philosophical analysis is the fact that propositions and questions which are really linguistic are often expressed in such a way that they appear to be factual.[1] A striking instance of this is provided by the proposition that a material thing cannot be in two places at once. This looks like an empirical proposition, and is constantly invoked by those who desire to prove that it is possible for an empirical proposition to be logically certain. But a more critical inspection shows that it is not empirical at all, but linguistic. It simply records the fact that, as the result of certain verbal conventions, the proposition that two sense-contents occur in the same visual or tactual sense-field is incompatible with the proposition that they belong to the same material thing.[2] And this is indeed a necessary fact. But it has not the least tendency to show that we have certain knowledge about the empirical properties of objects. For it is necessary only because we happen to use the relevant words in a particular way. There is no logical reason why we should not so alter our definitions that the sentence "A thing cannot be in two places at once" comes to express a self-contradiction instead of a necessary truth.

Another good example of linguistically necessary proposition which appears to be a record of empirical fact is the proposition, "Relations are not particulars, but universals." One might suppose that this was a proposition of the same order as, "Armenians are not Mohammedans, but Christians": but one would be mistaken. For, whereas the latter proposition is an empirical hypothesis relating to the religious practices of a certain group of people, the former is not a proposition about "things" at all, but simply about words. It records the fact that relation-symbols belong by definition to the class of symbols for characters, and not to the class of symbols for things.

The assertion that relations are universals provokes the question, "What is a universal?"; and this question is not, as it has traditionally been regarded, a question about the character of certain real objects, but a request for a definition of a certain term. Philosophy, as it is written, is full of questions like this,

[1] Carnap has stressed this point. Where we speak of "linguistic" propositions expressed in "factual" or "pseudo-factual" language he speaks of "Pseudo-Objektsätze" or "quasi-syntaktische Sätze" as being expressed in the "Inhalt-liche," as opposed to the "Formale Redeweise." Vide *Logische Syntax der Sprache*, Part V.

[2] cf. my article "On Particulars and Universals," *Proceedings of the Aristotelian Society*, *1933–4*, pp. 54, 55.

which seem to be factual but are not. Thus, to ask what is the nature of a material object is to ask for a definition of "material object," and this, as we shall shortly see, is to ask how propositions about material objects are to be translated into propositions about sense-contents. Similarly, to ask what is a number is to ask some such question as whether it is possible to translate propositions about the natural numbers into propositions about classes.[1] And the same thing applies to all the other philosophical questions of the form, "What is an x?" or, "What is the nature of x?" They are all requests for definitions, and, as we shall see, for definitions of a peculiar sort.

Although it is misleading to write about linguistic questions in "factual" language, it is often convenient for the sake of brevity. And we shall not always avoid doing it ourselves. But it is important that no one should be deceived by this practice into supposing that the philosopher is engaged on an empirical or a metaphysical enquiry. We may speak loosely of him as analysing facts, or notions, or even things. But we must make it clear that these are simply ways of saying that he is concerned with the definition of the corresponding words.

CHAPTER III

THE NATURE OF PHILOSOPHICAL ANALYSIS

From our assertion that philosophy provides definitions, it must not be inferred that it is the function of the philosopher to compile a dictionary, in the ordinary sense. For the definitions which philosophy is required to provide are of a different kind from those which we expect to find in dictionaries. In a dictionary we look mainly for what may be called *explicit* definitions; in philosophy, for definitions *in use*. A brief explanation should suffice to make the nature of this distinction clear.

We define a symbol *explicitly* when we put forward another symbol, or symbolic expression which is synonymous with it. And

[1] cf. Rudolf Carnap, *Logische Syntax der Sprache*, Part V, 79B, and 84.

the word "synonymous" is here used in such a way that two symbols belonging to the same language can be said to be synonymous if, and only if, the simple substitution of one symbol for the other, in any sentence in which either can significantly occur, always yields a new sentence which is equivalent to the old. And we say that two sentences of the same language are equivalent if, and only if, every sentence which is entailed by any given group of sentences in conjunction with one of them is entailed by the same group in conjunction with the other. And, in this usage of the word "entail," a sentence *s* is said to entail a sentence *t* when the proposition expressed by *t* is deducible from the proposition expressed by *s*; while a proposition *p* is said to be deducible from, or to follow from, a proposition *q* when the denial of *p* contradicts the assertion of *q*.

The provision of these criteria enables us to see that the vast majority of the definitions which are given in ordinary discourse are *explicit* definitions. In particular, it is worth remarking that the process of defining *per genus et differentiam*, to which Aristotelian logicians devote so much attention, always yields definitions which are explicit in the foregoing sense. Thus, when we define an oculist as an eye-doctor, what we are asserting is that, in the English language, the two symbols "oculist" and "eye-doctor" are synonymous. And, generally speaking, all the questions that are discussed by logicians in connection with this mode of definition are concerned with the possible ways of finding synonyms in a given language for any given term. We shall not enter into these questions ourselves, because they are irrelevant to our present purpose, which is to expound the method of philosophy. For the philosopher, as we have already said, is primarily concerned with the provision, not of *explicit* definitions, but of definitions *in use*.[1]

We define a symbol *in use*, not by saying that it is synonymous with some other symbol, but by showing how the sentences in which it significantly occurs can be translated into equivalent sentences, which contain neither the *definiendum* itself, nor any of its synonyms. A good illustration of this process is provided by Bertrand Russell's so-called theory of definite descriptions, which is not a theory at all in the ordinary sense, but an indication of,

[1] That this statement needs to be qualified is shown in the Introduction, pp. 24 *ff*.

the way in which all phrases of the form "the so-and-so" are to be defined.[1] It proclaims that every sentence which contains a symbolic expression of this form can be translated into a sentence which does not contain any such expression, but does contain a sub-sentence asserting that one, and only one, object possesses a certain property, or else that no one object possesses a certain property. Thus, the sentence "The round square cannot exist" is equivalent to "No one thing can be both square and round"; and the sentence "The author of *Waverley* was Scotch" is equivalent to "One person, and one person only, wrote *Waverley*, and that person was Scotch."[2] The first of these examples provides us with a typical illustration of the way in which any definite descriptive phrase which occurs as the subject of a negative existential sentence can be eliminated; and the second, with a typical illustration of the way in which any definite descriptive phrase which occurs anywhere in any other type of sentence can be eliminated. Together, therefore, they show us how to express what is expressed by any sentence which contains a definite descriptive phrase without employing any such phrase. And thus they furnish us with a definition of these phrases in use.

The effect of this definition of descriptive phrases, as of all good definitions, is to increase our understanding of certain sentences. And this is a benefit which the author of such a definition confers not only on others, but also on himself. It might be objected that he must already understand the sentences in order to be able to define the symbols which occur in them. But this initial understanding need not amount to anything more than an ability to tell, in practice, what sort of situations verify the propositions they express. Such an understanding of sentences containing definite descriptive phrases may be possessed even by those who believe that there are subsistent entities, such as the round square, or the present King of France. But the fact that they do maintain this shows that their understanding of these sentences is imperfect. For their lapse into metaphysics is the outcome of the naïve assumption that definite descriptive phrases are demonstrative symbols. And in the light of the clearer understanding which is afforded by Russell's definition, we see that this assumption is false. Nor could this end have been achieved by an explicit

[1] Vide *Principia Mathematica*, Introduction, Chapter iii, and *Introduction to Mathematical Philisophy*, Chapter xvi.
[2] This is not quite accurate, vide Introduction, pp. 22–4.

definition of any descriptive phrase. What was required was a translation of sentences containing such phrases which would reveal what may be called their logical complexity. In general, we may say that it is the purpose of a philosophical definition to dispel those confusions which arise from our imperfect understanding of certain types of sentence in our language, where the need cannot be met by the provision of a synonym for any symbol, either because there is no synonym, or else because the available synonyms are unclear in the same fashion as the symbol to which the confusion is due.

A complete philosophical elucidation of any language would consist, first, in enumerating the types of sentence that were significant in that language, and then in displaying the relations of equivalence that held between sentences of various types. And here it may be explained that two sentences are said to be of the same type when they can be correlated in such a way that to each symbol in one sentence there corresponds a symbol of the same type in the other; and that two symbols are said to be of the same type when it is always possible to substitute one for the other without changing a significant sentence into a piece of nonsense. Such a system of definitions in use would reveal what may be called the structure of the language in question. And thus we may regard any particular philosophical "theory," such as Russell's "theory of definite descriptions," as a revelation of part of the structure of a given language. In Russell's case, the language is the everyday English language; and any other language, such as French or German, which has the same structure as English.[1] And, in this context, it is not necessary to draw a distinction between the spoken and the written language. As far as the validity of a philosophical definition is concerned, it does not matter whether we regard the symbol defined as being constituted by visible marks or by sounds.

A factor which complicates the structure of a language such as English is the prevalence of ambiguous symbols. A symbol is said to be ambiguous when it is constituted by signs which are identical in their sensible form, not only with one another, but also with signs which are elements of some other symbol. For what makes two signs elements of the same symbol is not merely an

[1] This must not be taken to imply that all English-speaking people actually employ a single, precise system of symbols. Vide pp. 70–1.

identity of form, but also an identity of usage. Thus, if we were guided merely by the form of the sign, we should assume that the "is" which occurs in the sentence "He is the author of that book" was the same symbol as the "is" which occurs in the sentence "A cat is a mammal." But, when we come to translate the sentences, we find that the first is equivalent to "He, and no one else, wrote that book," and the second to "The class of mammals contains the class of cats." And this shows that, in this instance, each "is" is an ambiguous symbol which must not be confused with the other, nor with the ambiguous symbols of existence, and class-membership, and identity, and entailment, which are also constituted by signs of the form "is."

To say that a symbol is constituted by signs which are identical with one another in their sensible form, and in their significance, and that a sign is a sense-content, or a series of sense-contents, which is used to convey literal meaning, is not to say that a symbol is a collection, or system, of sense-contents. For when we speak of certain objects, b, c, d . . . as being elements of an object e, and of e as being constituted by b, c, d . . . we are not saying that they form part of e, in the sense in which my arm is a part of my body, or a particular set of books on my shelf is part of my collection of books. What we are saying is that all the sentences in which the symbol e occurs can be translated into sentences which do not contain e itself, or any symbol which is synonymous with e, but do contain symbols b, c, d . . . In such a case we say that e is a logical construction out of b, c, d . . . And, in general, we may explain the nature of logical constructions by saying that the introduction of symbols which denote logical constructions is a device which enables us to state complicated propositions about the elements of these constructions in a relatively simple form.

What one must not say is that logical constructions are fictitious objects. For while it is true that the English State, for example, is a logical construction out of individual people, and that the table at which I am writing is a logical construction out of sense-contents, it is not true that either the English State or this table is fictitious, in the sense in which Hamlet or a mirage is fictitious. Indeed, the assertion that tables are logical constructions out of sense-contents is not a factual assertion at all, in the sense in which the assertion that tables were fictitious objects would be a factual assertion, albeit a false one. It is, as our explanation of the notion of a logical construction should have made clear, a linguistic assertion, to the effect that the symbol "table" is definable in terms of certain symbols which stand for sense-contents. not explicitly, but in use. And this, as we have seen, is tantamount to saying that sentences which contain the symbol "table," or the corresponding symbol in any language which has the same structure as English, can all be translated into sentences of the same language which do not contain that symbol, nor any of its synonyms, but do contain certain symbols which stand for sense-contents; a fact which may be loosely expressed by saying that to say anything about a table is always to say something about sense-contents. This does not, of course, imply that to say something about a table is ever to say the same thing about the relevant sense-contents. For example, the sentence, "I am now sitting in front of a table" can, in principle, be translated into a sentence which does not mention tables, but only sense-contents. But this does not mean that we can simply substitute a sense-content symbol for the symbol "table" in the original sentence. If we do this, our new sentence, so far from being equivalent to the old, will be a mere piece of nonsense. To obtain a sentence which is equivalent to the sentence about the table, but refers to sense-contents instead, the whole of the original sentence has to be altered. And this, indeed, is implied by the fact that to say that tables are logical constructions out of sense-contents is to say, not that the symbol "table" can be explicitly defined in terms of symbols which stand for sense-contents, but only that it can be so defined in use. For, as we have seen, the function of a definition in use is not to provide us with a synonym for any symbol, but to enable us to translate sentences of a certain type.

The problem of giving an actual rule for translating sentences about a material thing into sentences about sense-contents, which may be called the problem of the "reduction" of material things to sense-contents, is the main philosophical part of the traditional problem of perception. It is true that writers on perception who set out to describe "the nature of a material thing" believe themselves to be discussing a factual question. But, as we have already pointed out, this is a mistake. The question, "What is the nature of a material thing?" is, like any other question of that form, a linguistic question, being a demand for a definition. And the propositions which are set forth in answer to it are linguistic propositions, even though they may be expressed in such a way that they seem to be factual. They are propositions about the relationship of symbols, and not about the properties of the things which the symbols denote.

It is necessary to emphasise this point in connection with the "problem of perception," since the fact that we are unable, in our everyday language, to describe the properties of sense-contents with any great precision, for lack of the requisite symbols, makes it convenient to give the solution of this problem in factual terminology. We express the fact that to speak about material things is, for each of us, a way of speaking about sense-contents, by saying that each of us "constructs" material things out of sense-contents: and we reveal the relationship between the two sorts of symbols by showing what are the principles of this "construction." In other words, one answers the question, "What is the nature of a material thing?" by indicating, in general terms, what are the relations that must hold between any two of one's sense-contents for them to be elements of the same material thing. The difficulty, which here seems to arise, of reconciling the subjectivity of sense-contents with the objectivity of material things will be dealt with in a later chapter of this book.[1]

The solution which we shall now give of this "problem of perception" will serve as a further illustration of the method of philosophical analysis. To simplify the question, we introduce the following definitions. We say that two sense-contents directly resemble one another when there is either no difference, or only an infinitesimal difference, of quality between them; and that they resemble one another indirectly when they are linked by a series of direct resemblances, but are not themselves directly resemblant, a relationship whose possibility depends on the fact that the relative product[2] of infinitesimal differences in quality is an appreciable difference in quality. And we say that two visual, or tactual, sense-contents are directly continuous when they belong to successive members of a series of actual, or possible, sense-fields, and there is no difference, or only an infinitesimal difference, between them, with respect to the position of each in

[1] Chapter VII.

[2] "The *relative product* of two relations R and S is the relation which holds between x and z when there is an intermediate term y such that x has the relation R to y and y has the relation S to z." *Principia Mathematica*, Introduction, Chapter I.

its own sense-field; and that they are indirectly continuous when they are related by an actual, or possible, series of such direct continuities. And here it should be explained that to say of a sense-experience, or a sense-field which is a part of a sense-experience, or a sense-content which is a part of a sense-field, that it is possible, as opposed to actual, is to say, not that it ever has occurred or will occur in fact, but that it would occur if certain specifiable conditions were fulfilled. So when it is said that a material thing is constituted by both actual and possible sense-contents, all that is being asserted is that the sentences referring to sense-contents, which are the translations of the sentences referring to any material thing, are both categorical and hypothetical. And thus the notion of a possible sense-content, or sense-experience, is as unobjectionable as the familiar notion of a hypothetical statement.

Relying on these preliminary definitions, one may assert with regard to any two of one's visual sense-contents, or with regard to any two of one's tactual sense-contents, that they are elements of the same material thing if, and only if, they are related to one another by a relation of direct, or indirect, resemblance in certain respects, and by a relation of direct, or indirect, continuity. And as each of these relations is symmetrical—that is to say, a relation which cannot hold between any terms A and B without also holding between B and A—and also transitive—that is, a relation which cannot hold between a term A and another term B, and between B and another term C, without holding between A and C—it follows that the groups of visual and tactual sense-contents which are constituted by means of these relations cannot have any members in common. And this means that no visual, or tactual, sense-content can be an element of more than one material thing.

The next step in the analysis of the notion of a material thing is to show how these separate groups of visual and tactual sense-contents are correlated. And this may be effected by saying that any two of one's visual and tactual groups belong to the same material thing when every element of the visual group which is of minimal visual depth forms part of the same sense-experience as an element of the tactual group which is of minimal tactual depth. We cannot here define visual or tactual depth otherwise than ostensively. The depth of a visual or tactual sense-content

66

is as much a sensible property of it as its length or breadth.[1] But we may describe it by saying that one visual or tactual sense-content has a greater depth than another when it is farther from the observer's body, provided that we make it clear that this is not intended to be a definition. For it would clearly vitiate any "reduction" of material things to sense-contents if the defining sentences contained references to human bodies, which are themselves material things. We, however, are obliged to mention material things when we wish to describe certain sense-contents, because the poverty of our language is such that we have no other verbal means of explaining what their properties are.

As for the sense-contents of taste, or sound, or smell, which are assigned to particular material things, they may be classified by reference to their association with tactual sense-contents. Thus, we assign sense-contents of taste to the same material things as the simultaneously occurring sense-contents of touch which are experienced by the palate, or the tongue. And in assigning an auditory or olfactory sense-content to a material thing, we remark that it is a member of a possible series of temporarily continuous sounds, or smells, of uniform quality but gradually increasing intensity; the series, namely, which one would ordinarily be said to experience in the course of moving towards the place from which the sound, or the smell, came; and we assign it to the same material thing as the tactual sense-content which is experienced at the same time as the sound, or the smell, of maximum intensity in the series.

What is next required of us, who are attempting to analyse the notion of a material thing, is the provision of a rule for translating sentences which refer to the "real" qualities of material things. Our answer is that to say of a certain quality that it is the real quality of a given material thing is to say that it characterises those elements of the thing which are the most conveniently measured of all the elements which possess qualities of the kind in question. Thus, when I look at a coin and assert that it is really round in shape, I am not asserting that the shape of the sense-content, which is the element of the coin that I am actually observing, is round, still less that the shape of all the visual, or tactual, elements of the coin is round; what I am asserting is that roundness of shape characterises those elements of the coin

[1] See H. H. Price, *Perception*, p. 218.

which are experienced from the point of view from which measurements of shape are most conveniently carried out. And similarly I assert that the real colour of the paper on which I am writing is white, even though it may not always appear to be white, because whiteness of colour characterises those visual elements of the paper which are experienced in the conditions in which the greatest discrimination of colours is possible. And, finally, we define relations of quality, or position, between material things in terms of the relations of quality, or position, which obtain between such "privileged" elements.

This definition, or, rather, this outline of a definition, of symbols which stand for material things is intended to have the same sort of effect as the definition of descriptive phrases which we gave as our original example of the process of philosophical analysis. It serves to increase our understanding of the sentences in which we refer to material things. In this case also, there is, of course, a sense in which we already understand such sentences. Those who use the English language have no difficulty, in practice, in identifying the situations which determine the truth or falsehood of such simple statements as "This is a table," or "Pennies are round." But they may very well be unaware of the hidden logical complexity of such statements which our analysis of the notion of a material thing has just brought to light. And, as a result, they may be led to adopt some metaphysical belief, such as the belief in the existence of material substances or invisible substrata, which is a source of confusion in all their speculative thought. And the utility of the philosophical definition which dispels such confusions is not to be measured by the apparent triviality of the sentences which it translates.

It is sometimes said that the purpose of such philosophical definitions is to reveal the meaning of certain symbols, or combinations of symbols. The objection to this way of speaking is that it does not give an unequivocal description of the philosopher's practice, because it employs, in "meaning," a highly ambiguous symbol. It is for this reason that we defined the relation of equivalence between sentences, without referring to "meaning." And, indeed, I doubt whether all the sentences which are equivalent, according to our definition, would ordinarily be said to have the same meaning. For I think that although a complex sign of the form "the sentences s and t have

68

the same meaning" is sometimes used, or taken, to express what we express by saying "the sentences s and t are equivalent," this is not the way in which such a sign is most commonly used or interpreted. I think that if we are to use the sign "meaning" in the way in which it is most commonly used, we must not say that two sentences have the same meaning for anyone, unless the occurrence of one always has the same effect on his thoughts and actions as the occurrence of the other. And, clearly, it is possible for two sentences to be equivalent, by our criterion, without having the same effect on anyone who employs the language. For instance, "p is a law of nature" is equivalent to "p is a general hypothesis which can always be relied on": but the associations of the symbol "law" are such that the former sentence tends to produce a very different psychological effect from its equivalent. It gives rise to a belief in the orderliness of nature, and even in the existence of a power "behind" that orderliness, which is not evoked by the equivalent sentence, and has, indeed, no rational warrant. Thus there are many people for whom these sentences do, in this common sense of "meaning," have different meanings. And this, I suspect, accounts for the widespread reluctance to admit that the laws of nature are merely hypotheses, just as the failure of some philosophers to recognise that material things are reducible to sense-contents is very largely due to the fact that no sentence which refers to sense-contents ever has the same psychological effect on them as a sentence which refers to a material thing. But, as we have seen, this is not a valid ground for denying that any two such sentences are equivalent.

Accordingly, one should avoid saying that philosophy is concerned with the meaning of symbols, because the ambiguity of "meaning" leads the undiscerning critic to judge the result of a philosophical enquiry by a criterion which is not applicable to it, but only to an empirical enquiry concerning the psychological effect which the occurrence of certain symbols has on a certain group of people. Such empirical enquiries are, indeed, an important element in sociology and in the scientific study of a language; but they are quite distinct from the logical enquiries which constitute philosophy.

It is misleading, also, to say, as some do, that philosophy tells us how certain symbols are actually used. For this suggests that the propositions of philosophy are factual propositions concerning the behaviour of a certain group of people; and this is not the case. The philosopher who asserts that, in the English language, the sentence "The author of *Waverley* was Scotch" is equivalent to "One person, and one person only, wrote *Waverley*, and that person was Scotch" is not asserting that all, or most, English-speaking people use these sentences interchangeably. What he is asserting is that, in virtue of certain rules of entailment, namely those which are characteristic of "correct" English, every sentence which is entailed by "The author of *Waverley* was Scotch," in conjunction with any given group of sentences, is entailed also by that group, in conjunction with "One person, and one person only, wrote *Waverley*, and that person was Scotch." That English-speaking people should employ the verbal conventions that they do is, indeed, an empirical fact. But the deduction of relations of equivalence from the rules of entailment which characterise the English, or any other, language is a purely logical activity; and it is in this logical activity, and not in any empirical study of the linguistic habits of any group of people, that philosophical analysis consists.[1]

Thus, in specifying the language to which he intends his definitions to apply, the philosopher is simply describing the conventions from which his definitions are deduced; and the validity of the definitions depends solely on their compatibility with these conventions. In most cases, indeed, the definitions are obtained from conventions which do, in fact, correspond to the conventions which are actually observed by some group of people. And it is a necessary condition of the utility of the definitions, as a means of clarification, that this should be so. But it is a mistake to suppose that the existence of such a correspondence is ever part of what the definitions actually assert.[2]

It is to be remarked that the process of analysing a language is facilitated if it is possible to use for the classification of its forms

[1] There is a ground for saying that the philosopher is always concerned with an artificial language. For the conventions which we follow in our actual usage of words are not altogether systematic and precise.

[2] Thus if I wish to refute a philosophical opponent I do not argue about people's linguistic habits. I try to prove that his definitions involve a contradiction. Suppose, for example, that he is maintaining that "A is a free agent" is equivalent to "A's actions are uncaused." Then I refute him by getting him to admit that "A is a free agent" is entailed by "A is morally responsible for his actions" whereas "A's actions are uncaused" entails "A is not morally responsible for his actions."

an artificial system of symbols whose structure is known. The best-known example of such a symbolism is the so-called system of logistic which was employed by Russell and Whitehead in their *Principia Mathematica*. But it is not necessary that the language in which analysis is carried out should be different from the language analysed. If it were, we should be obliged to suppose, as Russell once suggested, "that every language has a structure concerning which, *in the language*, nothing can be said, but that there may be another language dealing with the structure of the first language, and having itself a new structure, and that to this hierarchy of languages there may be no limit."[1] This was written presumably in the belief that an attempt to refer to the structure of a language in the language itself would lead to the occurrence of logical paradoxes.[2] But Carnap, by actually carrying out such an analysis, has subsequently shown that a language can without self-contradiction be used in the analysis of itself.[3]

CHAPTER IV

THE *A PRIORI*

THE VIEW OF PHILOSOPHY which we have adopted may, I think, fairly be described as a form of empiricism. For it is characteristic of an empiricist to eschew metaphysics, on the ground that every factual proposition must refer to sense-experience. And even if the conception of philosophizing as an activity of analysis is not to be discovered in the traditional theories of empiricists, we have seen that it is implicit in their practice. At the same time, it must be made clear that, in calling ourselves empiricists, we are not avowing a belief in any of the psychological doctrines which are commonly associated with empiricism. For, even if these doctrines were valid, their validity would be independent of the validity of any philosophical thesis. It could

[1] Introduction to L. Wittgenstein's *Tractatus Logico-Philosophicus*, p. 23.
[2] Concerning logical paradoxes, see Russell and Whitehead, *Principia Mathematica*, Introduction, Chapter ii; F. P. Ramsey, *Foundations of Mathematics*, pp. 1–63; and Lewis and Langford, *Symbolic Logic*, Chapter xiii.
[3] Vide *Logische Syntax der Sprache*, Parts I and II.

be established only by observation, and not by the purely logical considerations upon which our empiricism rests.

Having admitted that we are empiricists, we must now deal with the objection that is commonly brought against all forms of empiricism; the objection, namely, that it is impossible on empiricist principles to account for our knowledge of necessary truths. For, as Hume conclusively showed, no general proposition whose validity is subject to the test of actual experience can ever be logically certain. No matter how often it is verified in practice, there still remains the possibility that it will be confuted on some future occasion. The fact that a law has been substantiated in $n-1$ cases affords no logical guarantee that it will be substantiated in the nth case also, no matter how large we take n to be. And this means that no general proposition referring to a matter of fact can ever be shown to be necessarily and universally true. It can at best be a probable hypothesis. And this, we shall find, applies not only to general propositions, but to all propositions which have a factual content. They can none of them ever become logically certain. This conclusion, which we shall elaborate later on, is one which must be accepted by every consistent empiricist. It is often thought to involve him in complete scepticism; but this is not the case. For the fact that the validity of a proposition cannot be logically guaranteed in no way entails that it is irrational for us to believe it. On the contrary, what is irrational is to look for a guarantee where none can be forthcoming; to demand certainty where probability is all that is obtainable. We have already remarked upon this, in referring to the work of Hume. And we shall make the point clearer when we come to treat of probability, in explaining the use which we make of empirical propositions. We shall discover that there is nothing perverse or paradoxical about the view that all the "truths" of science and common sense are hypotheses; and consequently that the fact that it involves this view constitutes no objection to the empiricist thesis.

Where the empiricist does encounter difficulty is in connection with the truths of formal logic and mathematics. For whereas a scientific generalisation is readily admitted to be fallible, the truths of mathematics and logic appear to everyone to be necessary and certain. But if empiricism is correct no proposition which has a factual content can be necessary or certain. Accordingly

∴ also
Metaphysical
statements

the empiricist must deal with the truths of logic and mathematics in one of the two following ways: he must say either that they are not necessary truths, in which case he must account for the universal conviction that they are; or he must say that they have no factual content, and then he must explain how a proposition which is empty of all factual content can be true and useful and surprising.

If neither of these courses proves satisfactory, we shall be obliged to give way to rationalism. We shall be obliged to admit that there are some truths about the world which we can know independently of experience; that there are some properties which we can ascribe to all objects, even though we cannot conceivably observe that all objects have them. And we shall have to accept it as a mysterious inexplicable fact that our thought has this power to reveal to us authoritatively the nature of objects which we have never observed. Or else we must accept the Kantian explanation which, apart from the epistemological difficulties which we have already touched on, only pushes the mystery a stage further back.

It is clear that any such concession to rationalism would upset the main argument of this book. For the admission that there were some facts about the world which could be known independently of experience would be incompatible with our fundamental contention that a sentence says nothing unless it is empirically verifiable. And thus the whole force of our attack on metaphysics would be destroyed. It is vital, therefore, for us to be able to show that one or other of the empiricist accounts of the propositions of logic and mathematics is correct. If we are successful in this, we shall have destroyed the foundations of rationalism. For the fundamental tenet of rationalism is that thought is an independent source of knowledge, and is moreover a more trustworthy source of knowledge than experience; indeed some rationalists have gone so far as to say that thought is the only source of knowledge. And the ground for this view is simply that the only necessary truths about the world which are known to us are known through thought and not through experience. So that if we can show either that the truths in question are not necessary or that they are not "truths about the world," we shall be taking away the support on which rationalism rests. We shall be making good the empiricist contention that there are no "truths of reason" which refer to matters of fact.

The course of maintaining that the truths of logic and mathematics are not necessary or certain was adopted by Mill. He maintained that these propositions were inductive generalizations based on an extremely large number of instances. The fact that the number of supporting instances was so very large accounted, in his view, for our believing these generalizations to be necessarily and universally true. The evidence in their favour was so strong that it seemed incredible to us that a contrary instance should ever arise. Nevertheless it was in principle possible for such generalizations to be confuted. They were highly probable, but, being inductive generalizations, they were not certain. The difference between them and the hypotheses of natural science was a difference in degree and not in kind. Experience gave us very good reason to suppose that a "truth" of mathematics or logic was true universally; but we were not possessed of a guarantee. For these "truths" were only empirical hypotheses which had worked particularly well in the past; and, like all empirical hypotheses, they were theoretically fallible.

I do not think that this solution of the empiricist's difficulty with regard to the propositions of logic and mathematics is acceptable. In discussing it, it is necessary to make a distinction which is perhaps already enshrined in Kant's famous dictum that, although there can be no doubt that all our knowledge begins with experience, it does not follow that it all arises out of experience.[1] When we say that the truths of logic are known independently of experience, we are not of course saying that they are innate, in the sense that we are born knowing them. It is obvious that mathematics and logic have to be learned in the same way as chemistry and history have to be learned. Nor are we denying that the first person to discover a given logical or mathematical truth was led to it by an inductive procedure. It is very probable, for example, that the principle of the syllogism was formulated not before but after the validity of syllogistic reasoning had been observed in a number of particular cases. What we are discussing, however, when we say that logical and mathematical truths are known independently of experience, is not a historical question concerning the way in which these truths were originally discovered, nor a psychological question concerning the way in which each of us comes to learn them, but an epistemological

[1] *Critique of Pure Reason*, 2nd ed., Introduction, section i.

question. The contention of Mill's which we reject is that the propositions of logic and mathematics have the same status as empirical hypotheses; that their validity is determined in the same way. We maintain that they are independent of experience in the sense that they do not owe their validity to empirical verification. We may come to discover them through an inductive process; but once we have apprehended them we see that they are necessarily true, that they hold good for every conceivable instance. And this serves to distinguish them from empirical generalizations. For we know that a proposition whose validity depends upon experience cannot be seen to be necessarily and universally true.

In rejecting Mill's theory, we are obliged to be somewhat dogmatic. We can do no more than state the issue clearly and then trust that his contention will be seen to be discrepant with the relevant logical facts. The following considerations may serve to show that of the two ways of dealing with logic and mathematics which are open to the empiricist, the one which Mill adopted is not the one which is correct.

The best way to substantiate our assertion that the truths of formal logic and pure mathematics are necessarily true is to examine cases in which they might seem to be confuted. It might easily happen, for example, that when I came to count what I had taken to be five pairs of objects, I found that they amounted only to nine. And if I wished to mislead people I might say that on this occasion twice five was not ten. But in that case I should not be using the complex sign "$2 \times 5 = 10$" in the way in which it is ordinarily used. I should be taking it not as the expression of a purely mathematical proposition, but as the expression of an empirical generalization, to the effect that whenever I counted what appeared to me to be five pairs of objects I discovered that they were ten in number. This generalization may very well be false. But if it proved false in a given case, one would not say that the mathematical proposition "$2 \times 5 = 10$" had been confuted. One would say that I was wrong in supposing that there were five pairs of objects to start with, or that one of the objects had been taken away while I was counting, or that two of them had coalesced, or that I had counted wrongly. One would adopt as an explanation whatever empirical hypothesis fitted in best with the accredited facts. The one explanation which would in no circumstances be adopted is that ten is not always the product of two and five.

To take another example: if what appears to be a Euclidean triangle is found by measurement not to have angles totalling 180 degrees, we do not say that we have met with an instance which invalidates the mathematical proposition that the sum of the three angles of a Euclidean triangle is 180 degrees. We say that we have measured wrongly, or, more probably, that the triangle we have been measuring is not Euclidean. And this is our procedure in every case in which a mathematical truth might appear to be confuted. We always preserve its validity by adopting some other explanation of the occurrence.

The same thing applies to the principles of formal logic. We may take an example relating to the so-called law of excluded middle, which states that a proposition must be either true or false, or, in other words, that it is impossible that a proposition and its contradictory should neither of them be true. One might suppose that a proposition of the form "x has stopped doing y" would in certain cases constitute an exception to this law. For instance, if my friend has never yet written to me, it seems fair to say that it is neither true nor false that he has stopped writing to me. But in fact one would refuse to accept such an instance as an invalidation of the law of excluded middle. One would point out that the proposition "My friend has stopped writing to me" is not a simple proposition, but the conjunction of the two propositions "My friend wrote to me in the past" and "My friend does not write to me now": and, furthermore, that the proposition "My friend has not stopped writing to me" is not, as it appears to be, contradictory to "My friend has stopped writing to me," but only contrary to it. For it means "My friend wrote to me in the past, and he still writes to me." When, therefore, we say that such a proposition as "My friend has stopped writing to me" is sometimes neither true nor false, we are speaking inaccurately. For we seem to be saying that neither it nor its contradictory is true. Whereas what we mean, or anyhow should mean, is that neither it nor its apparent contradictory is true. And its apparent contradictory is really only its contrary. Thus we preserve the law of excluded middle by showing that the negating of a sentence does not always yield the contradictory of the proposition originally expressed.

76

There is no need to give further examples. Whatever instance *(Previous stuff)* we care to take, we shall always find that the situations in which a logical or mathematical principle might appear to be confuted are accounted for in such a way as to leave the principle unassailed. And this indicates that Mill was wrong in supposing that a situation could arise which would overthrow a mathematical truth. The principles of logic and mathematics are true universally simply because we never allow them to be anything else. And the reason for this is that we cannot abandon them without contradicting ourselves, without sinning against the rules which govern the use of language, and so making our utterances self-stultifying. In other words, the truths of logic and mathematics are analytic propositions or tautologies. In saying this we are making what will be held to be an extremely controversial statement, and we must now proceed to make its implications clear.

The most familiar definition of an analytic proposition, or judgement, as he called it, is that given by Kant. He said[1] that an analytic judgement was one in which the predicate B belonged to the subject A as something which was covertly contained in the concept of A. He contrasted analytic with synthetic judgements, in which the predicate B lay outside the subject A, although it did stand in connection with it. Analytic judgements, he explains, "add nothing through the predicate to the concept of the subject, but merely break it up into those constituent concepts that have all along been thought in it, although confusedly." Synthetic judgements, on the other hand, "add to the concept of the subject a predicate which has not been in any wise thought in it, and which no analysis could possibly extract from it." Kant gives "all bodies are extended" as an example of an analytic judgement, on the ground that the required predicate can be extracted from the concept of "body," "in accordance with the principle of contradiction"; as an example of a synthetic judgement, he gives "all bodies are heavy." He refers also to "$7+5=12$" as a synthetic judgement, on the ground that the concept of twelve is by no means already thought in merely thinking the union of seven and five. And he appears to regard this as tantamount to saying that the judgement does not rest on the principle of contradiction alone. He holds, also, that through analytic judgements our knowledge is not extended as it is

[1] *Critique of Pure Reason*, 2nd ed., Introduction, sections iv and v.

77

through synthetic judgements. For in analytic judgements "the concept which I already have is merely set forth and made intelligible to me."

I think that this is a fair summary of Kant's account of the distinction between analytic and synthetic propositions, but I do not think that it succeeds in making the distinction clear. For even if we pass over the difficulties which arise out of the use of the vague term "concept," and the unwarranted assumption that every judgement, as well as every German or English sentence, can be said to have a subject and a predicate, there remains still this crucial defect. Kant does not give one straightforward criterion for distinguishing between analytic and synthetic propositions; he gives two distinct criteria, which are by no means equivalent. Thus his ground for holding that the proposition "$7+5 = 12$" is synthetic is, as we have seen, that the subjective intension of "$7+5$" does not comprise the subjective intension of "12"; whereas his ground for holding that "all bodies are extended" is an analytic proposition is that it rests on the principle of contradiction alone. That is, he employs a psychological criterion in the first of these examples, and a logical criterion in the second, and takes their equivalence for granted. But, in fact, a proposition which is synthetic according to the former criterion may very well be analytic according to the latter. For, as we have already pointed out, it is possible for symbols to be synonymous without having the same intensional meaning for anyone: and accordingly from the fact that one can think of the sum of seven and five without necessarily thinking of twelve, it by no means follows that the proposition "$7+5 = 12$" can be denied without self-contradiction. From the rest of his argument, it is clear that it is this logical proposition, and not any psychological proposition, that Kant is really anxious to establish. His use of the psychological criterion leads him to think that he has established it, when he has not.

I think that we can preserve the logical import of Kant's distinction between analytic and synthetic propositions, while avoiding the confusions which mar his actual account of it, if we say that a proposition is analytic when its validity depends solely on the definitions of the symbols it contains, and synthetic when its validity is determined by the facts of experience. Thus, the proposition "There are ants which have established a system of slavery" is a synthetic proposition. For we

78

cannot tell whether it is true or false merely by considering the definitions of the symbols which constitute it. We have to resort to actual observation of the behaviour of ants. On the other hand, the proposition "Either some ants are parasitic or none are" is an analytic proposition. For one need not resort to observation to discover that there either are or are not ants which are parasitic. If one knows what is the function of the words "either," "or," and "not," then one can see that any proposition of the form "Either p is true or p is not true" is valid, independently of experience. Accordingly, all such propositions are analytic.

It is to be noticed that the proposition "Either some ants are parasitic or none are" provides no information whatsoever about the behaviour of ants, or, indeed, about any matter of fact. And this applies to all analytic propositions. They none of them provide any information about any matter of fact. In other words, they are entirely devoid of factual content. And it is for this reason that no experience can confute them.

When we say that analytic propositions are devoid of factual content, and consequently that they say nothing, we are not suggesting that they are senseless in the way that metaphysical utterances are senseless. For, although they give us no information about any empirical situation, they do enlighten us by illustrating the way in which we use certain symbols. Thus if I say, "Nothing can be coloured in different ways at the same time with respect to the same part of itself," I am not saying anything about the properties of any actual thing; but I am not talking nonsense. I am expressing an analytic proposition, which records our determination to call a colour expanse which differs in quality from a neighbouring colour expanse a different part of a given thing. In other words, I am simply calling attention to the implications of a certain linguistic usage. Similarly, in saying that if all Bretons are Frenchmen, and all Frenchmen Europeans, then all Bretons are Europeans, I am not describing any matter of fact. But I am showing that in the statement that all Bretons are Frenchmen, and all Frenchmen Europeans, the further statement that all Bretons are Europeans is implicitly contained. And I am thereby indicating the convention which governs our usage of the words "if" and "all."

We see, then, that there is a sense in which analytic propositions do give us new knowledge. They call attention to linguistic usages, of which we might otherwise not be conscious, and they reveal unsuspected implications in our assertions and beliefs. But we can see also that there is a sense in which they may be said to add nothing to our knowledge. For they tell us only what we may be said to know already. Thus, if I know that the existence of May Queens is a relic of tree-worship, and I discover that May Queens still exist in England, I can employ the tautology "If p implies q, and p is true, q is true" to show that there still exists a relic of tree-worship in England. But in saying that there are still May Queens in England, and that the existence of May Queens is a relic of tree-worship, I have already asserted the existence in England of a relic of tree-worship. The use of the tautology does, indeed, enable me to make this concealed assertion explicit. But it does not provide me with any new knowledge, in the sense in which empirical evidence that the election of May Queens had been forbidden by law would provide me with new knowledge. If one had to set forth all the information one possessed, with regard to matters of fact, one would not write down any analytic propositions. But one would make use of analytic propositions in compiling one's encyclopædia, and would thus come to include propositions which one would otherwise have overlooked. And, besides enabling one to make one's list of information complete, the formulation of analytic propositions would enable one to make sure that the synthetic propositions of which the list was composed formed a self-consistent system. By showing which ways of combining propositions resulted in contradictions, they would prevent one from including incompatible propositions and so making the list self-stultifying. But in so far as we had actually used such words as "all" and "or" and "not" without falling into self-contradiction, we might be said already to know what was revealed in the formulation of analytic propositions illustrating the rules which govern our usage of these logical particles. So that here again we are justified in saying that analytic propositions do not increase our knowledge.

The analytic character of the truths of formal logic was obscured in the traditional logic through its being insufficiently formalized. For in speaking always of judgements, instead of propositions, and introducing irrelevant psychological questions, the traditional logic gave the impression of being concerned in some specially intimate way with the workings of thought. What it was actually concerned with was the formal relationship of classes, as is shown by the fact that all its principles of inference are subsumed in the Boolean class-calculus, which is subsumed in its turn in the propositional calculus of Russell and Whitehead.[1] Their system, expounded in *Principia Mathematica*, makes it clear that formal logic is not concerned with the properties of men's minds, much less with the properties of material objects, but simply with the possibility of combining propositions by means of logical particles into analytic propositions, and with studying the formal relationship of these analytic propositions, in virtue of which one is deducible from another. Their procedure is to exhibit the propositions of formal logic as a deductive system, based on five primitive propositions, subsequently reduced in number to one. Hereby the distinction between logical truths and principles of inference, which was maintained in the Aristotelian logic, very properly disappears. Every principle of inference is put forward as a logical truth and every logical truth can serve as a principle of inference. The three Aristotelian "laws of thought," the law of identity, the law of excluded middle, and the law of non-contradiction, are incorporated in the system, but they are not considered more important than the other analytic propositions. They are not reckoned among the premises of the system. And the system of Russell and Whitehead itself is probably only one among many possible logics, each of which is composed of tautologies as interesting to the logician as the arbitrarily selected Aristotelian "laws of thought."[2]

A point which is not sufficiently brought out by Russell, if indeed it is recognised by him at all, is that every logical proposition is valid in its own right. Its validity does not depend on its being incorporated in a system, and deduced from certain propositions which are taken as self-evident. The construction of systems of logic is useful as a means of discovering and certifying analytic propositions, but it is not in principle essential even for this purpose. For it is possible to conceive of a symbolism in which every analytic proposition could be seen to be analytic in virtue of its form alone.

The fact that the validity of an analytic proposition in no way

[1] Vide Karl Menger, "Die Neue Logik," *Krise und Neuaufbau in den Exakten Wissenschaften*, pp. 94–6; and Lewis and Langford, *Symbolic Logic*, Chapter v.

[2] Vide Lewis and Langford, *Symbolic Logic*, Chapter vii, for an elaboration of this point.

depends on its being deducible from other analytic propositions is our justification for disregarding the question whether the propositions of mathematics are reducible to propositions of formal logic, in the way that Russell supposed.[1] For even if it is the case that the definition of a cardinal number as a class of classes similar to a given class is circular, and it is not possible to reduce mathematical notions to purely logical notions, it will still remain true that the propositions of mathematics are analytic propositions. They will form a special class of analytic propositions, containing special terms, but they will be none the less analytic for that. For the criterion of an analytic proposition is that its validity should follow simply from the definition of the terms contained in it, and this condition is fulfilled by the propositions of pure mathematics.

The mathematical propositions which one might most pardonably suppose to be synthetic are the propositions of geometry. For it is natural for us to think, as Kant thought, that geometry is the study of the properties of physical space, and consequently that its propositions have factual content. And if we believe this, and also recognise that the truths of geometry are necessary and certain, then we may be inclined to accept Kant's hypothesis that space is the form of intuition of our outer sense, a form imposed by us on the matter of sensation, as the only possible explanation of our *a priori* knowledge of these synthetic propositions. But while the view that pure geometry is concerned with physical space was plausible enough in Kant's day, when the geometry of Euclid was the only geometry known, the subsequent invention of non-Euclidean geometries has shown it to be mistaken. We see now that the axioms of a geometry are simply definitions, and that the theorems of a geometry are simply the logical consequences of these definitions.[2] A geometry is not in itself about physical space; in itself it cannot be said to be "about" anything. But we can use a geometry to reason about physical space. That is to say, once we have given the axioms a physical interpretation, we can proceed to apply the theorems to the objects which satisfy the axioms. Whether a geometry can be applied to the actual physical world or not, is an empirical question which falls outside the scope of the geometry itself. There is no sense, therefore, in asking

[1] Vide *Introduction to Mathematical Philosophy*, Chapter ii.

[2] cf. H. Poincaré, *La Science et l'Hypothèse*, Part II, Chapter iii.

which of the various geometries known to us are false and which are true. In so far as they are all free from contradiction, they are all true. What one can ask is which of them is the most useful on any given occasion, which of them can be applied most easily and most fruitfully to an actual empirical situation. But the proposition which states that a certain application of a geometry is possible is not itself a proposition of that geometry. All that the geometry itself tells us is that if anything can be brought under the definitions, it will also satisfy the theorems. It is therefore a purely logical system, and its propositions are purely analytic propositions.

It might be objected that the use made of diagrams in geometrical treatises shows that geometrical reasoning is not purely abstract and logical, but depends on our intuition of the properties of figures. In fact, however, the use of diagrams is not essential to completely rigorous geometry. The diagrams are introduced as an aid to our reason. They provide us with a particular application of the geometry, and so assist us to perceive the more general truth that the axioms of the geometry involve certain consequences. But the fact that most of us need the help of an example to make us aware of those consequences does not show that the relation between them and the axioms is not a purely logical relation. It shows merely that our intellects are unequal to the task of carrying out very abstract processes of reasoning without the assistance of intuition. In other words, it has no bearing on the nature of geometrical propositions, but is simply an empirical fact about ourselves. Moreover, the appeal to intuition, though generally of psychological value, is also a source of danger to the geometer. He is tempted to make assumptions which are accidentally true of the particular figure he is taking as an illustration, but do not follow from his axioms. It has, indeed, been shown that Euclid himself was guilty of this, and consequently that the presence of the figure is essential to some of his proofs.[1] This shows that his system is not, as he presents it, completely rigorous, although of course it can be made so. It does not show that the presence of the figure is essential to a truly rigorous geometrical proof. To suppose that it did would be to take as a necessary feature of all geometries what is really only an incidental defect in one particular geometrical system.

[1] cf. M. Black, *The Nature of Mathematics*, p. 154.

We conclude, then, that the propositions of pure geometry are analytic. And this leads us to reject Kant's hypothesis that geometry deals with the form of intuition of our outer sense. For the ground for this hypothesis was that it alone explained how the propositions of geometry could be both true *a priori* and synthetic: and we have seen that they are not synthetic. Similarly our view that the propositions of arithmetic are not synthetic but analytic leads us to reject the Kantian hypothesis[1] that arithmetic is concerned with our pure intuition of time, the form of our inner sense. And thus we are able to dismiss Kant's transcendental æsthetic without having to bring forward the epistemological difficulties which it is commonly said to involve. For the only argument which can be brought in favour of Kant's theory is that it alone explains certain "facts." And now we have found that the "facts" which it purports to explain are not facts at all. For while it is true that we have *a priori* knowledge of necessary propositions, it is not true, as Kant supposed, that any of these necessary propositions are synthetic. They are without exception analytic propositions, or, in other words, tautologies.

We have already explained how it is that these analytic propositions are necessary and certain. We saw that the reason why they cannot be confuted in experience is that they do not make any assertion about the empirical world. They simply record our determination to use words in a certain fashion. We cannot deny them without infringing the conventions which are presupposed by our very denial, and so falling into self-contradiction. And this is the sole ground of their necessity. As Wittgenstein puts it, our justification for holding that the world could not conceivably disobey the laws of logic is simply that we could not say of an unlogical world how it would look.[2] And just as the validity of an analytic proposition is independent of the nature of the external world; so is it independent of the nature of our minds. It is perfectly conceivable that we should have employed different linguistic conventions from those which we actually do employ. But whatever these conventions might be, the tautologies in which we recorded them would always be necessary. For any denial of them would be self-stultifying.

[1] This hypothesis is not mentioned in the *Critique of Pure Reason*, but was maintained by Kant at an earlier date.

[2] *Tractatus Logico-Philosophicus*, 3·031.

We see, then, that there is nothing mysterious about the apodeictic certainty of logic and mathematics. Our knowledge that no observation can ever confute the proposition "$7+5=12$" depends simply on the fact that the symbolic expression "$7+5$" is synonymous with "12," just as our knowledge that every oculist is an eye-doctor depends on the fact that the symbol "eye-doctor" is synonymous with "oculist." And the same explanation holds good for every other *a priori* truth.

What is mysterious at first sight is that these tautologies should on occasion be so surprising, that there should be in mathematics and logic the possibility of invention and discovery. As Poincaré says: "If all the assertions which mathematics puts forward can be derived from one another by formal logic, mathematics cannot amount to anything more than an immense tautology. Logical inference can teach us nothing essentially new, and if everything is to proceed from the principle of identity, everything must be reducible to it. But can we really allow that these theorems which fill so many books serve no other purpose than to say in a roundabout fashion '$A=A$'?"[1] Poincaré finds this incredible. His own theory is that the sense of invention and discovery in mathematics belongs to it in virtue of mathematical induction, the principle that what is true for the number 1, and true for $n+1$ when it is true for n,[2] is true for all numbers. And he claims that this is a synthetic *a priori* principle. It is, in fact, *a priori*, but it is not synthetic. It is a defining principle of the natural numbers, serving to distinguish them from such numbers as the infinite cardinal numbers, to which it cannot be applied.[3] Moreover, we must remember that discoveries can be made, not only in arithmetic, but also in geometry and formal logic, where no use is made of mathematical induction. So that even if Poincaré were right about mathematical induction, he would not have provided a satisfactory explanation of the paradox that a mere body of tautologies can be so interesting and so surprising.

The true explanation is very simple. The power of logic and mathematics to surprise us depends, like their usefulness, on the limitations of our reason. A being whose intellect was infinitely

---

[1] *La Science et l'Hypothèse*, Part I, Chapter i.

[2] This was wrongly stated in previous editions as "true for n when it is true for $n+1$."

[3] cf. B. Russell's *Introduction to Mathematical Philosophy*, Chapter iii, p. 27.

powerful would take no interest in logic and mathematics.[1] For he would be able to see at a glance everything that his definitions implied, and, accordingly, could never learn anything from logical inference which he was not fully conscious of already. But our intellects are not of this order. It is only a minute proportion of the consequences of our definitions that we are able to detect at a glance. Even so simple a tautology as "$91 \times 79 = 7189$" is beyond the scope of our immediate apprehension. To assure ourselves that "7189" is synonymous with "91×79" we have to resort to calculation, which is simply a process of tautological transformation—that is, a process by which we change the form of expressions without altering their significance. The multiplication tables are rules for carrying out this process in arithmetic, just as the laws of logic are rules for the tautological transformation of sentences expressed in logical symbolism or in ordinary language. As the process of calculation is carried out more or less mechanically, it is easy for us to make a slip and so unwittingly contradict ourselves. And this accounts for the existence of logical and mathematical "falsehoods," which otherwise might appear paradoxical. Clearly the risk of error in logical reasoning is proportionate to the length and the complexity of the process of calculation. And in the same way, the more complex an analytic proposition is, the more chance it has of interesting and surprising us.

It is easy to see that the danger of error in logical reasoning can be minimized by the introduction of symbolic devices, which enable us to express highly complex tautologies in a conveniently simple form. And this gives us an opportunity for the exercise of invention in the pursuit of logical enquiries. For a well-chosen definition will call our attention to analytic truths, which would otherwise have escaped us. And the framing of definitions which are useful and fruitful may well be regarded as a creative act.

Having thus shown that there is no inexplicable paradox involved in the view that the truths of logic and mathematics are all of them analytic, we may safely adopt it as the only satisfactory explanation of their *a priori* necessity. And in adopting it we vindicate the empiricist claim that there can be no *a priori*

---

[1] cf. Hans Hahn, "Logik, Mathematik und Naturerkennen," *Einheitswissenschaft*, Heft II, p. 18. "Ein allwissendes Wesen braucht keine Logik und keine Mathematik."

knowledge of reality. For we show that the truths of pure reason, the propositions which we know to be valid independently of all experience, are so only in virtue of their lack of factual content. To say that a proposition is true *a priori* is to say that it is a tautology. And tautologies, though they may serve to guide us in our empirical search for knowledge, do not in themselves contain any information about any matter of fact.

CHAPTER V

TRUTH AND PROBABILITY

Having shown how the validity of *a priori* propositions is determined, we shall now put forward the criterion which is used to determine the validity of empirical propositions. In this way we shall complete our theory of truth. For it is easy to see that the purpose of a "theory of truth" is simply to describe the criteria by which the validity of the various kinds of propositions is determined. And as all propositions are either empirical or *a priori*, and we have already dealt with the *a priori*, all that is now required to complete our theory of truth is an indication of the way in which we determine the validity of empirical propositions. And this we shall shortly proceed to give.

But first of all we ought, perhaps, to justify our assumption that the object of a "theory of truth" can only be to show how propositions are validated. For it is commonly supposed that the business of the philosopher who concerns himself with "truth" is to answer the question "What is truth?" and that it is only an answer to this question that can fairly be said to constitute a "theory of truth." But when we come to consider what this famous question actually entails, we find that it is not a question which gives rise to any genuine problem; and consequently that no theory can be required to deal with it.

We have already remarked that all questions of the form, "What is the nature of x?" are requests for a definition of a symbol in use, and that to ask for a definition of a symbol x in use is to ask how the sentences in which x occurs are to be translated into equivalent sentences, which do not contain x or any of its synonyms. Applying this to the case of "truth" we find that to ask, "What is truth?" is to ask for such a translation of the sentence "(the proposition) p is true."

It may be objected here that we are ignoring the fact that it is not merely propositions that can be said to be true or false, but also statements and assertions and judgements and assumptions and opinions and beliefs. But the answer to this is that to say that a belief, or a statement, or a judgement, is true is always an elliptical way of ascribing truth to a proposition, which is believed, or stated, or judged. Thus, if I say that the Marxist's belief that capitalism leads to war is true, what I am saying is that the proposition, believed by Marxists, that capitalism leads to war is true; and the illustration holds good when the word "opinion" or "assumption," or any of the others in the list, is substituted for the word "belief." And, further, it must be made clear that we are not hereby committing ourselves to the metaphysical doctrine that propositions are real entities.[1] Regarding classes as a species of logical constructions, we may define a proposition as a class of sentences which have the same intensional significance for anyone who understands them. Thus, the sentences, "I am ill," "Ich bin krank," "Je suis malade," are all elements of the proposition "I am ill." And what we have previously said about logical constructions should make it clear that we are not asserting that a proposition is a collection of sentences, but rather that to speak about a given proposition is a way of speaking about certain sentences, just as to speak about sentences, in this usage, is a way of speaking about particular signs.

Reverting to the analysis of truth, we find that in all sentences of the form "p is true," the phrase "is true" is logically superfluous. When, for example, one says that the proposition "Queen Anne is dead" is true, all that one is saying is that Queen Anne is dead. And similarly, when one says that the proposition "Oxford is the capital of England" is false, all that one is saying is that Oxford is not the capital of England. Thus, to say that a proposition is true is just to assert it, and to say that it is false is just to assert its contradictory. And this indicates that the terms "true" and "false" connote nothing, but function in the sentence

[1] For a criticism of this doctrine, see G. Ryle, "Are there propositions?" *Aristotelian Society Proceedings, 1929–30.*

simply as marks of assertion and denial. And in that case there can be no sense in asking us to analyse the concept of "truth."

This point seems almost too obvious to mention, yet the pre-occupation of philosophers with the "problem of truth" shows that they have overlooked it. Their excuse is that references to truth generally occur in sentences whose grammatical forms suggest that the word "true" does stand for a genuine quality or relation. And a superficial consideration of these sentences might lead one to suppose that there was something more in the question "What is truth?" than a demand for the analysis of the sentence "p is true." But when one comes to analyse the sentences in question, one always finds that they contain sub-sentences of the form "p is true" or "p is false," and that when they are translated in such a way as to make these sub-sentences explicit, they contain no other mention of truth. Thus, to take two typical examples, the sentence "A proposition is not made true by being believed" is equivalent to "for no value of p or x, is 'p is true' entailed by 'x believes p' ": and the sentence "Truth is sometimes stranger than fiction" is equivalent to "There are values of p and q such that p is true and q is false and p is more surprising than q." And the same result would be yielded by any other example one cared to take. In every case the analysis of the sentence would confirm our assumption that the question "What is truth?" is reducible to the question "What is the analysis of the sentence 'p is true'?" And it is plain that this question raises no genuine problem, since we have shown that to say that p is true is simply a way of asserting p.[1]

We conclude, then, that there is no problem of truth as it is ordinarily conceived. The traditional conception of truth as a "real quality" or a "real relation" is due, like most philosophical mistakes, to a failure to analyse sentences correctly. There are sentences, such as the two we have just analysed, in which the word "truth" seems to stand for something real; and this leads the speculative philosopher to enquire what this "something" is. Naturally he fails to obtain a satisfactory answer, since his question is illegitimate. For our analysis has shown that the word "truth" does not stand for anything, in the way which such a question requires.

[1] cf. F. P. Ramsey on "Facts and Propositions," *The Foundations of Mathematics*, pp. 142–3.

It follows that if all theories of truth were theories about the "real quality" or the "real relation," which the word "truth" is naïvely supposed to stand for, they would be all nonsense. But in fact they are for the most part theories of an entirely different sort. Whatever question their authors may think that they are discussing, what they are really discussing most of the time is the question "What makes a proposition true or false?" And this is a loose way of expressing the question "With regard to any proposition p, what are the conditions in which p (is true) and what are the conditions in which not-p?" In other words, it is a way of asking how propositions are validated. And this is the question which we were considering when we embarked on our digression about the analysis of truth.

In saying that we propose to show "how propositions are validated," we do not of course mean to suggest that all propositions are validated in the same way. On the contrary we lay stress on the fact that the criterion by which we determine the validity of an *a priori* or analytic proposition is not sufficient to determine the validity of an empirical or synthetic proposition. For it is characteristic of empirical propositions that their validity is not purely formal. To say that a geometrical proposition, or a system of geometrical propositions, is false is to say that it is self-contradictory. But an empirical proposition, or a system of empirical propositions, may be free from contradiction, and still be false. It is said to be false, not because it is formally defective, but because it fails to satisfy some material criterion. And it is our business to discover what this criterion is.

We have been assuming so far that empirical propositions, though they differ from *a priori* propositions in their method of validation, do not differ in this respect among themselves. Having found that all *a priori* propositions are validated in the same way, we have taken it for granted that this holds good of empirical propositions also. But this assumption would be challenged by a great many philosophers who agree with us in most other respects.[1] They would say that among empirical propositions, there was a special class of propositions whose validity consisted in the fact that they directly recorded an immediate experience.

[1] e.g. M. Schlick, "Über das Fundament der Erkenntnis," *Erkenntnis*, Band IV, Heft II; and "Facts and Propositions," *Analysis*, Vol. II, No. 5; and B. von Juhos, "Empiricism and Physicalism," *Analysis*, Vol. II, No. 6.

They maintain that these propositions, which we may call "ostensive" propositions, are not mere hypotheses but are absolutely certain. For they are supposed to be purely demonstrative in character, and so incapable of being refuted by any subsequent experience. And they are, on this view, the only empirical propositions which are certain. The rest are hypotheses which derive what validity they have from their relationship to the ostensive propositions. For their probability is held to be determined by the number and variety of the ostensive propositions which can be deduced from them.

That no synthetic proposition which is not purely ostensive can be logically indubitable, may be granted without further ado. What we cannot admit is that any synthetic proposition can be purely ostensive.[1] For the notion of an ostensive proposition appears to involve a contradiction in terms. It implies that there could be a sentence which consisted of purely demonstrative symbols and was at the same time intelligible. And this is not even a logical possibility. A sentence which consisted of demonstrative symbols would not express a genuine proposition. It would be a mere ejaculation, in no way characterizing that to which it was supposed to refer.[2]

The fact is that one cannot in language point to an object without describing it. If a sentence is to express a proposition, it cannot merely name a situation; it must say something about it. And in describing a situation, one is not merely "registering" a sense-content; one is classifying it in some way or other, and this means going beyond what is immediately given. But a proposition would be ostensive only if it recorded what was immediately experienced, without referring in any way beyond. And as this is not possible, it follows that no genuine synthetic proposition can be ostensive, and consequently that none can be absolutely certain.

Accordingly we hold not merely that no ostensive propositions ever are expressed, but that it is inconceivable that any ostensive proposition ever should be expressed. That no ostensive propositions ever are expressed might be admitted even by those who

[1] See also Rudolf Carnap, "Über Protokolsätze," *Erkenntnis*, Band III; Otto Neurath, "Protokolsätze," *Erkenntnis*, Band III; and "Radikaler Physikalismus und 'Wirkliche Welt,'" *Erkenntnis*, Band IV, Heft V; and Carl Hempel, "On the Logical Positivists' Theory of Truth," *Analysis*, Vol. II, No. 4.
[2] This question is reviewed in the Introduction, pp. 10–11.

believe in them. They might allow that in actual practice one never limits oneself to describing the qualities of an immediately presented sense-content, but always treats it as if it were a material thing. And it is obvious that the propositions in which we formulate our ordinary judgements about material things are not ostensive, referring as they do to an infinite series of actual and possible sense-contents. But it is in principle possible to formulate propositions which simply describe the qualities of sense-contents without expressing perceptual judgements. And it is claimed that these artificial propositions would be genuinely ostensive. It should be clear from what we have already said that this claim is unjustified. And if any doubt on this point still remains, we may remove it with the help of an example.

Let us suppose that I assert the proposition "This is white," and my words are taken to refer, not, as they normally would, to some material thing, but to a sense-content. Then what I am saying about this sense-content is that it is an element in the class of sense-contents which constitutes "white" for me; or in other words that it is similar in colour to certain other sense-contents, namely those which I should call, or actually have called, white. And I think I am saying also that it corresponds in some fashion to the sense-contents which go to constitute "white" for other people: so that if I discovered that I had an abnormal colour-sense, I should admit that the sense-content in question was not white. But even if we exclude all reference to other people, it is still possible to think of a situation which would lead me to suppose that my classification of a sense-content was mistaken. I might, for example, have discovered that whenever I sensed a sense-content of a certain quality, I made some distinctive overt bodily movement; and I might on one occasion be presented with a sense-content which I asserted to be of that quality, and then fail to make the bodily reaction which I had come to associate with it. In such a case I should probably abandon the hypothesis that sense-contents of that quality always called out in me the bodily reaction in question. But I should not, logically, be obliged to abandon it. If I found it more convenient, I could save this hypothesis by assuming that I really did make the reaction, although I did not notice it, or, alternatively, that the sense-content did not have the quality I asserted it to have. The fact that this course is a possible one, that it involves no logical contradiction, proves that a proposition which describes the quality of a presented sense-content may as legitimately be doubted as any other empirical proposition.[1] And this shows that such a proposition is not ostensive, for we have seen that an ostensive proposition could not legitimately be doubted. But propositions describing the actual qualities of presented sense-contents are the only examples of ostensive propositions which those who believe in ostensive propositions have ever ventured to give. And if these propositions are not ostensive, it is certain that none are.

In denying the possibility of ostensive propositions, we are not of course denying that there really is a "given" element in each of our sense-experiences. Nor are we suggesting that our sensations are themselves doubtful. Indeed such a suggestion would be nonsensical. A sensation is not the sort of thing which can be doubtful or not doubtful. A sensation simply occurs. What are doubtful are the propositions which refer to our sensations, including the propositions which describe the qualities of a presented sense-content, or assert that a certain sense-content has occurred. To identify a proposition of this sort with the sensation itself would clearly be a gross logical blunder. Yet I fancy that the doctrine of ostensive propositions is the outcome of such a tacit identification. It is difficult to account for it in any other way.[2]

However, we shall not waste time speculating about the origins of this false philosophical doctrine. Such questions may be left to the historian. Our business is to show that the doctrine is false, and this we may fairly claim to have done. It should now be clear that there are no absolutely certain empirical propositions. It is only tautologies that are certain. Empirical propositions are one

[1] Of course those who believe in "ostensive" propositions do not maintain that such a proposition as "This is white" is valid in virtue of its form alone. What they assert is that I am entitled to regard the proposition "This is white" as objectively certain when I am actually experiencing a white sense-content. But can it really be the case that they mean to assert no more than the trivial tautology that when I am seeing something white, then I am seeing something white? See following footnote.

[2] It has subsequently occurred to me that the doctrine of ostensive propositions may be due to the confusion of the proposition "It is certain that p implies p"—e.g. "It is certain that if I am in pain, then I am in pain"— which is a tautology, with the proposition "p implies that (p is certain)"— e.g. "If I am in pain, then the proposition 'I am in pain' is certain," which is, in general, false. Vide my article on "The Criterion of Truth," *Analysis*, Vol. III, Nos. 1 and 2.

and all hypotheses, which may be confirmed or discredited in actual sense-experience. And the propositions in which we record the observations that verify these hypotheses are themselves hypotheses which are subject to the test of further sense-experience. Thus there are no final propositions. When we set about verifying a hypothesis we may make an observation which satisfies us at the time. But the very next moment we may doubt whether the observation really did take place, and require a fresh process of verification in order to be reassured. And, logically, there is no reason why this procedure should not continue indefinitely, each act of verification supplying us with a new hypothesis, which in turn leads to a further series of acts of verification. In practice we assume that certain types of observation are trustworthy, and admit the hypothesis that they have occurred without bothering to embark on a process of verification. But we do this, not from obedience to any logical necessity, but from a purely pragmatic motive, the nature of which will shortly be explained.

When one speaks of hypotheses being verified in experience, it is important to bear in mind that it is never just a single hypothesis which an observation confirms or discredits, but always a system of hypotheses. Suppose that we have devised an experiment to test the validity of a scientific "law." The law states that in certain conditions a certain type of observation will always be forthcoming. It may happen in this particular instance that we make the observation as our law predicts. Then it is not only the law itself that is substantiated, but also the hypotheses which assert the existence of the requisite conditions. For it is only by assuming the existence of these conditions that we can hold that our observation is relevant to the law. Alternatively, we may fail to make the expected observation. And in that case we may conclude that the law is invalidated by our experiment. But we are not obliged to adopt this conclusion. If we wish to preserve our law, we may do so by abandoning one or more of the other relevant hypotheses. We may say that the conditions were really not what they seemed to be, and construct a theory to explain how we came to be mistaken about them; or we may say that some factor which we had dismissed as irrelevant was really relevant, and support this view with supplementary hypotheses. We may even assume that the experiment was really not unfavourable, and that our negative observation was hallucinatory.

And in that case we must bring the hypotheses which record the conditions that are deemed necessary for the occurrence of a hallucination into line with the hypotheses which describe the conditions in which this observation is supposed to have taken place. Otherwise we shall be maintaining incompatible hypotheses. And this is the one thing that we may not do. But, so long as we take suitable steps to keep our system of hypotheses free from self-contradiction, we may adopt any explanation of our observations that we choose. In practice our choice of an explanation is guided by certain considerations, which we shall presently describe. And these considerations have the effect of limiting our freedom in the matter of preserving and rejecting hypotheses. But logically our freedom is unlimited. Any procedure which is self-consistent will satisfy the requirements of logic.

It appears, then, that the "facts of experience" can never compel us to abandon a hypothesis. A man can always sustain his convictions in the face of apparently hostile evidence if he is prepared to make the necessary *ad hoc* assumptions. But although any particular instance in which a cherished hypothesis appears to be refuted can always be explained away, there must still remain the possibility that the hypothesis will ultimately be abandoned. Otherwise it is not a genuine hypothesis. For a proposition whose validity we are resolved to maintain in the face of any experience is not a hypothesis at all, but a definition. In other words, it is not a synthetic but an analytic proposition.

That some of our most hallowed "laws of nature" are merely disguised definitions is, I think, incontestable, but this is not a question that we can go into here.[1] It is sufficient for us to point out that there is a danger of mistaking such definitions for genuine hypotheses, a danger which is increased by the fact that the same form of words may at one time, or for one set of people, express a synthetic proposition, and at another time, or for another set of people, express a tautology. For our definitions of things are not immutable. And if experience leads us to entertain a very strong belief that everything of the kind A has the property of being a B, we tend to make the possession of this property a defining characteristic of the kind. Ultimately we may refuse to call anything A unless it is also a B. And in that case the sentence

[1] For an elaboration of this view, see H. Poincaré, *La Science et l'Hypothèse.*

"All A's are B's," which originally expressed a synthetic generalization, would come to express a plain tautology.

One good reason for drawing attention to this possibility is that the neglect of it by philosophers is responsible for much of the confusion that infects their treatment of general propositions. Consider the stock example, "All men are mortal." We are told that this is not a doubtful hypothesis, as Hume maintained, but an instance of a necessary connection. And if we ask what it is that is here necessarily connected, the only answer that appears possible to us is that it is the concept of "man" and the concept of "being mortal." But the only meaning which we attach to the statement that two concepts are necessarily connected is that the sense of one concept is contained in that of the other. Thus to say that "All men are mortal" is an instance of a necessary connection is to say that the concept of being mortal is contained in the concept of man, and this amounts to saying that "All men are mortal" is a tautology. Now the philosopher may use the word "man" in such a way that he would refuse to call anything a man unless it were mortal. And in that case the sentence "All men are mortal" will, as far as he is concerned, express a tautology. But this does not mean that the proposition which we ordinarily express by that sentence is a tautology. Even for our philosopher, it remains a genuine empirical hypothesis. Only he cannot now express it in the form, "All men are mortal." Instead, he must say that everything which has the other defining properties of a man also has the property of being mortal, or something to that effect. Thus we may create tautologies by a suitable adjustment of our definitions: but we cannot solve empirical problems merely by juggling with the meanings of words.

Of course, when a philosopher says that the proposition "All men are mortal" is an instance of a necessary connection, he does not intend to say that it is a tautology. It is left to us to point out that this is all he can be saying, if his words are to bear their ordinary sense and at the same time express a significant proposition. But I think that he finds it possible to hold that this general proposition is both synthetic and necessary, only because he identifies it tacitly with the tautology which might, given suitable conventions, be expressed by the same form of words. And the same applies to all other general propositions of law. We may turn the sentences which now express them into expressions of definitions. And then these sentences will express necessary propositions. But these will be different propositions from the original generalizations. They, as Hume saw, can never be necessary. However firmly we believe them, it is always conceivable that a future experience will lead us to abandon them.

This brings us once more to the question, What are the considerations that determine in any given situation which of the relevant hypotheses shall be preserved and which shall be abandoned? It is sometimes suggested that we are guided solely by the principle of economy, or, in other words, by our desire to make the least possible alteration in our previously accepted system of hypotheses. But though we undoubtedly have this desire, and are influenced by it to some extent, it is not the sole, or even the dominant, factor in our procedure. If our concern was simply to keep our existing system of hypotheses intact, we should not feel obliged to take any notice of an unfavourable observation. We should not feel the need to account for it in any way whatsoever —not even by introducing the hypothesis that we had just had a hallucination. We should simply ignore it. But, in fact, we do not disregard inconvenient observations. Their occurrence always causes us to make some alteration in our system of hypotheses in spite of our desire to keep it intact. Why is this so? If we can answer this question, and show why we find it necessary to alter our systems of hypotheses at all, we shall be in a better position to decide what are the principles according to which such alterations are actually carried out.

What we must do to solve this problem is to ask ourselves, What is the purpose of formulating hypotheses? Why do we construct these systems in the first place? The answer is that they are designed to enable us to anticipate the course of our sensations. The function of a system of hypotheses is to warn us beforehand what will be our experience in a certain field—to enable us to make accurate predictions. The hypotheses may therefore be described as rules which govern our expectation of future experience. There is no need to say why we require such rules. It is plain that on our ability to make successful predictions depends the satisfaction of even our simplest desires, including the desire to survive.

Now the essential feature of our procedure with regard to the formulation of these rules is the use of past experience as a guide to the future. We have already remarked upon this, when discussing the so-called problem of induction, and we have seen that there is no sense in asking for a theoretical justification of this policy. The philosopher must be content to record the facts of scientific procedure. If he seeks to justify it, beyond showing that it is self-consistent, he will find himself involved in spurious problems. This is a point which we stressed earlier on, and we shall not trouble to argue it over again.

We remark, then, as a fact that our forecasts of future experience are in some way determined by what we have experienced in the past. And this fact explains why science, which is essentially predictive, is also to some extent a description of our experience.[1] But it is noticeable that we tend to ignore those features of our experience which cannot be made the basis of fruitful generalizations. And, furthermore, that which we do describe, we describe with some latitude. As Poincaré puts it: "One does not limit oneself to generalizing experience, one corrects it; and the physicist who consented to abstain from these corrections and really be satisfied with bare experience would be obliged to promulgate the most extraordinary laws."[2]

But even if we do not follow past experience slavishly in making our predictions, we are guided by it to a very large extent. And this explains why we do not simply disregard the conclusion of an unfavourable experiment. We assume that a system of hypotheses which has broken down once is likely to break down again. We could, of course, assume that it had not broken down at all, but we believe that this assumption would not pay us so well as the recognition that the system had really failed us, and therefore required some alteration if it was not to fail us again. We alter our system because we think that by altering it we shall make it a more efficient instrument for the anticipation of experience. And this belief is derived from our guiding principle that, broadly speaking, the future course of our sensations will be in accordance with the past.

This desire of ours to have an efficient set of rules for our predictions, which causes us to take notice of unfavourable observations, is also the factor which primarily determines how we adjust our system to cover the new data. It is true that we are infected

[1] It will be seen that even "descriptions of past experience" are in a sense predictive since they function as "rules for the anticipation of future experience." See the end of this chapter for an elaboration of this point.

[2] *La Science et l'Hypothèse*, Part IV, Chapter ix, p. 170.

with a spirit of conservatism and would rather make small alterations than large ones. It is disagreeable and troublesome for us to admit that our existing system is radically defective. And it is true that, other things being equal, we prefer simple to complex hypotheses, again from the desire to save ourselves trouble. But if experience leads us to suppose that radical changes are necessary, then we are prepared to make them, even though they do complicate our system, as the recent history of physics shows. When an observation runs counter to our most confident expectations, the easiest course is to ignore it, or at any rate to explain it away. If we do not do this, it is because we think that, if we leave our system as it is, we shall suffer further disappointments. We think it will increase the efficiency of our system as an instrument of prediction if we make it compatible with the hypothesis that the unexpected observation occurred. Whether we are right in thinking this is a question which cannot be settled by argument. We can only wait and see if our new system is successful in practice. If it is not, we alter it once again.

We have now obtained the information we required in order to answer our original question, "What is the criterion by which we test the validity of an empirical proposition?" The answer is that we test the validity of an empirical hypothesis by seeing whether it actually fulfils the function which it is designed to fulfil. And we have seen that the function of an empirical hypothesis is to enable us to anticipate experience. Accordingly, if an observation to which a given proposition is relevant conforms to our expectations, the truth of that proposition is confirmed. One cannot say that the proposition has been proved absolutely valid, because it is still possible that a future observation will discredit it. But one can say that its probability has been increased. If the observation is contrary to our expectations, then the status of the proposition is jeopardised. We may preserve it by adopting or abandoning other hypotheses: or we may consider it to have been confuted. But even if it is rejected in consequence of an unfavourable observation, one cannot say that it has been invalidated absolutely. For it is still possible that future observations will lead us to reinstate it. One can say only that its probability has been diminished.

It is necessary now to make clear what is meant in this context by the term "probability." In referring to the probability of a proposition, we are not, as is sometimes supposed, referring to an intrinsic property of it, or even to an unanalysable logical relation which holds between it and other propositions. Roughly speaking, all that we mean by saying that an observation increases the probability of a proposition is that it increases our confidence in the proposition, as measured by our willingness to rely on it in practice as a forecast of our sensations, and to retain it in preference to other hypotheses in face of an unfavourable experience. And, similarly, to say of an observation that it diminishes the probability of a proposition is to say that it decreases our willingness to include the proposition in the system of accepted hypotheses which serve us as guides to the future.[1]

As it stands, this account of the notion of probability is somewhat over-simplified. For it assumes that we deal with all hypotheses in a uniform self-consistent fashion, and this is unfortunately not the case. In practice, we do not always relate belief to observation in the way which is generally recognized to be the most reliable. Although we acknowledge that certain standards of evidence ought always to be observed in the formation of our beliefs, we do not always observe them. In other words, we are not always rational. For to be rational is simply to employ a self-consistent accredited procedure in the formation of all one's beliefs. The fact that the procedure, by reference to which we now determine whether a belief is rational, may subsequently forfeit our confidence, does not in any way detract from the rationality of adopting it now. For we define a rational belief as one which is arrived at by the methods which we now consider reliable. There is no absolute standard of rationality, just as there is no method of constructing hypotheses which is guaranteed to be reliable. We trust the methods of contemporary science because they have been successful in practice. If in the future we were to adopt different methods, then beliefs which are now rational might become irrational from the standpoint of these new methods. But the fact that this is possible has no bearing on the fact that these beliefs are rational now.

This definition of rationality enables us to amend our account of what is meant by the term "probability," in the usage with which we are now concerned. To say that an observation increases

[1] This definition is not, of course, intended to apply to the mathematical usage of the term "probability."

the probability of a hypothesis is not always equivalent to saying that it increases the degree of confidence with which we actually entertain the hypothesis, as measured by our readiness to act upon it: for we may be behaving irrationally. It is equivalent to saying that the observation increases the degree of confidence with which it is rational to entertain the hypothesis. And here we may repeat that the rationality of a belief is defined, not by reference to any absolute standard, but by reference to part of our own actual practice.

The obvious objection to our original definition of probability was that it was incompatible with the fact that one is sometimes mistaken about the probability of a proposition—that one can believe it to be more or less probable than it really is. It is plain that our amended definition escapes this objection. For, according to it, the probability of a proposition is determined both by the nature of our observations and by our conception of rationality. So that when a man relates belief to observation in a way which is inconsistent with the accredited scientific method of evaluating hypotheses, it is compatible with our definition of probability to say that he is mistaken about the probability of the propositions which he believes.

With this account of probability we complete our discussion of the validity of empirical propositions. The point which we must finally stress is that our remarks apply to all empirical propositions without exception, whether they are singular, or, particular, or universal. Every synthetic proposition is a rule for the anticipation of future experience, and is distinguished in content from other synthetic propositions by the fact that it is relevant to different situations. So that the fact that propositions referring to the past have the same hypothetical character as those which refer to the present, and those which refer to the future, in no way entails that these three types of proposition are not distinct. For they are verified by, and so serve to predict, different experiences.

It may be their failure to appreciate this point which has caused certain philosophers to deny that propositions about the past are hypotheses in the same sense as the laws of a natural science are hypotheses. For they have not been able to support their view by any substantial arguments, or to say what propositions about the past are, if they are not hypotheses, of the sort we have just described. For my own part, I do not find anything excessively paradoxical in the view that propositions about the past are rules for the prediction of those "historical" experiences which are commonly said to verify them,[1] and I do not see how else "our knowledge of the past" is to be analysed. And I suspect, moreover, that those who object to our pragmatic treatment of history are really basing their objections on a tacit, or explicit, assumption that the past is somehow "objectively there" to be corresponded to—that it is "real" in the metaphysical sense of the term. And from what we have remarked concerning the metaphysical issue of idealism and realism, it is clear that such an assumption is not a genuine hypothesis.[2]

CHAPTER VI

CRITIQUE OF ETHICS AND THEOLOGY

THERE IS STILL one objection to be met before we can claim to have justified our view that all synthetic propositions are empirical hypotheses. This objection is based on the common supposition that our speculative knowledge is of two distinct kinds—that which relates to questions of empirical fact, and that which relates to questions of value. It will be said that "statements of value" are genuine synthetic propositions, but that they cannot with any show of justice be represented as hypotheses, which are used to predict the course of our sensations; and, accordingly, that the existence of ethics and æsthetics as branches of speculative knowledge presents an insuperable objection to our radical empiricist thesis.

In face of this objection, it is our business to give an account of "judgements of value" which is both satisfactory in itself and consistent with our general empiricist principles. We shall set ourselves to show that in so far as statements of value are

[1] The implications of this statement may be misleading, vide Introduction, p. 19.

[2] The case for a pragmatic treatment of history, in our sense, is well put by C. L. Lewis in *Mind and the World Order*, pp. 150–3.

significant, they are ordinary "scientific" statements; and that in so far as they are not scientific, they are not in the literal sense significant, but are simply expressions of emotion which can be neither true nor false. In maintaining this view, we may confine ourselves for the present to the case of ethical statements. What is said about them will be found to apply, *mutatis mutandis*, to the case of æsthetic statements also.[1]

The ordinary system of ethics, as elaborated in the works of ethical philosophers, is very far from being a homogeneous whole. Not only is it apt to contain pieces of metaphysics, and analyses of non-ethical concepts: its actual ethical contents are themselves of very different kinds. We may divide them, indeed, into four main classes. There are, first of all, propositions which express definitions of ethical terms, or judgements about the legitimacy or possibility of certain definitions. Secondly, there are propositions describing the phenomena of moral experience, and their causes. Thirdly, there are exhortations to moral virtue. And, lastly, there are actual ethical judgements. It is unfortunately the case that the distinction between these four classes, plain as it is, is commonly ignored by ethical philosophers; with the result that it is often very difficult to tell from their works what it is that they are seeking to discover or prove.

In fact, it is easy to see that only the first of our four classes, namely that which comprises the propositions relating to the definitions of ethical terms, can be said to constitute ethical philosophy. The propositions which describe the phenomena of moral experience, and their causes, must be assigned to the science of psychology, or sociology. The exhortations to moral virtue are not propositions at all, but ejaculations or commands which are designed to provoke the reader to action of a certain sort. Accordingly, they do not belong to any branch of philosophy or science. As for the expressions of ethical judgements, we have not yet determined how they should be classified. But inasmuch as they are certainly neither definitions nor comments upon definitions, nor quotations, we may say decisively that they do not belong to ethical philosophy. A strictly philosophical treatise on ethics should therefore make no ethical pronouncements. But it should, by giving an analysis of ethical terms, show

[1] The argument that follows should be read in conjunction with the Introduction, pp. 20–2.

what is the category to which all such pronouncements belong. And this is what we are now about to do.

A question which is often discussed by ethical philosophers is whether it is possible to find definitions which would reduce all ethical terms to one or two fundamental terms. But this question, though it undeniably belongs to ethical philosophy, is not relevant to our present enquiry. We are not now concerned to discover which term, within the sphere of ethical terms, is to be taken as fundamental; whether, for example, "good" can be defined in terms of "right" or "right" in terms of "good," or both in terms of "value." What we are interested in is the possibility of reducing the whole sphere of ethical terms to non-ethical terms. We are enquiring whether statements of ethical value can be translated into statements of empirical fact.

That they can be so translated is the contention of those ethical philosophers who are commonly called subjectivists, and of those who are known as utilitarians. For the utilitarian defines the rightness of actions, and the goodness of ends, in terms of the pleasure, or happiness, or satisfaction, to which they give rise; the subjectivist, in terms of the feelings of approval which a certain person, or group of people, has towards them. Each of these types of definition makes moral judgements into a sub-class of psychological or sociological judgements; and for this reason they are very attractive to us. For, if either was correct, it would follow that ethical assertions were not generically different from the factual assertions which are ordinarily contrasted with them; and the account which we have already given of empirical hypotheses would apply to them also.

Nevertheless we shall not adopt either a subjectivist or a utilitarian analysis of ethical terms. We reject the subjectivist view that to call an action right, or a thing good, is to say that it is generally approved of, because it is not self-contradictory to assert that some actions which are generally approved of are not right, or that some things which are generally approved of are not good. And we reject the alternative subjectivist view that a man who asserts that a certain action is right, or that a certain thing is good, is saying that he himself approves of it, on the ground that a man who confessed that he sometimes approved of what was bad or wrong would not be contradicting himself. And a similar argument is fatal to utilitarianism. We cannot agree that to call an action right is to say that of all the actions possible in the circumstances it would cause, or be likely to cause, the greatest happiness, or the greatest balance of pleasure over pain, or the greatest balance of satisfied over unsatisfied desire, because we find that it is not self-contradictory to say that it is sometimes wrong to perform the action which would actually or probably cause the greatest happiness, or the greatest balance of pleasure over pain, or of satisfied over unsatisfied desire. And since it is not self-contradictory to say that some pleasant things are not good, or that some bad things are desired, it cannot be the case that the sentence "x is good" is equivalent to "x is pleasant," or to "x is desired." And to every other variant of utilitarianism with which I am acquainted the same objection can be made. And therefore we should, I think, conclude that the validity of ethical judgements is not determined by the felicific tendencies of actions, any more than by the nature of people's feelings; but that it must be regarded as "absolute" or "intrinsic," and not empirically calculable.

If we say this, we are not, of course, denying that it is possible to invent a language in which all ethical symbols are definable in non-ethical terms, or even that it is desirable to invent such a language and adopt it in place of our own; what we are denying is that the suggested reduction of ethical to non-ethical statements is consistent with the conventions of our actual language. That is, we reject utilitarianism and subjectivism, not as proposals to replace our existing ethical notions by new ones, but as analyses of our existing ethical notions. Our contention is simply that, in our language, sentences which contain normative ethical symbols are not equivalent to sentences which express psychological propositions, or indeed empirical propositions of any kind.

It is advisable here to make it plain that it is only normative ethical symbols, and not descriptive ethical symbols, that are held by us to be indefinable in factual terms. There is a danger of confusing these two types of symbols, because they are commonly constituted by signs of the same sensible form. Thus a complex sign of the form "x is wrong" may constitute a sentence which expresses a moral judgement concerning a certain type of conduct, or it may constitute a sentence which states that a certain type of conduct is repugnant to the moral sense of a particular society. In the latter case, the symbol "wrong" is a descriptive ethical symbol, and the sentence in which it occurs expresses an ordinary sociological proposition; in the former case, the symbol "wrong" is a normative ethical symbol, and the sentence in which it occurs does not, we maintain, express an empirical proposition at all. It is only with normative ethics that we are at present concerned; so that whenever ethical symbols are used in the course of this argument without qualification, they are always to be interpreted as symbols of the normative type.

In admitting that normative ethical concepts are irreducible to empirical concepts, we seem to be leaving the way clear for the "absolutist" view of ethics—that is, the view that statements of value are not controlled by observation, as ordinary empirical propositions are, but only by a mysterious "intellectual intuition." A feature of this theory, which is seldom recognized by its advocates, is that it makes statements of value unverifiable. For it is notorious that what seems intuitively certain to one person may seem doubtful, or even false, to another. So that unless it is possible to provide some criterion by which one may decide between conflicting intuitions, a mere appeal to intuition is worthless as a test of a proposition's validity. But in the case of moral judgements, no such criterion can be given. Some moralists claim to settle the matter by saying that they "know" that their own moral judgements are correct. But such an assertion is of purely psychological interest, and has not the slightest tendency to prove the validity of any moral judgement. For dissentient moralists may equally well "know" that their ethical views are correct. And, as far as subjective certainty goes, there will be nothing to choose between them. When such differences of opinion arise in connection with an ordinary empirical proposition, one may attempt to resolve them by referring to, or actually carrying out, some relevant empirical test. But with regard to ethical statements, there is, on the "absolutist" or "intuitionist" theory, no relevant empirical test. We are therefore justified in saying that on this theory ethical statements are held to be unverifiable. They are, of course, also held to be genuine synthetic propositions.

Considering the use which we have made of the principle that a synthetic proposition is significant only if it is empirically verifiable, it is clear that the acceptance of an "absolutist" theory of ethics would undermine the whole of our main argument. And as we have already rejected the "naturalistic" theories which are commonly supposed to provide the only alternative to "absolutism" in ethics, we seem to have reached a difficult position. We shall meet the difficulty by showing that the correct treatment of ethical statements is afforded by a third theory, which is wholly compatible with our radical empiricism.

We begin by admitting that the fundamental ethical concepts are unanalysable, inasmuch as there is no criterion by which one can test the validity of the judgements in which they occur. So far we are in agreement with the absolutists. But, unlike the absolutists, we are able to give an explanation of this fact about ethical concepts. We say that the reason why they are unanalysable is that they are mere pseudo-concepts. The presence of an ethical symbol in a proposition adds nothing to its factual content. Thus if I say to someone, "You acted wrongly in stealing that money," I am not stating anything more than if I had simply said, "You stole that money." In adding that this action is wrong I am not making any further statement about it. I am simply evincing my moral disapproval of it. It is as if I had said, "You stole that money," in a peculiar tone of horror, or written it with the addition of some special exclamation marks. The tone, or the exclamation marks, adds nothing to the literal meaning of the sentence. It merely serves to show that the expression of it is attended by certain feelings in the speaker.

If now I generalise my previous statement and say, "Stealing money is wrong," I produce a sentence which has no factual meaning—that is, expresses no proposition which can be either true or false. It is as if I had written "Stealing money!!"—where the shape and thickness of the exclamation marks show, by a suitable convention, that a special sort of moral disapproval is the feeling which is being expressed. It is clear that there is nothing said here which can be true or false. Another man may disagree with me about the wrongness of stealing, in the sense that he may not have the same feelings about stealing as I have, and he may quarrel with me on account of my moral sentiments. But he cannot, strictly speaking, contradict me. For in saying that a certain type of action is right or wrong, I am not making any factual statement, not even a statement about my own state of mind. I am merely expressing certain moral sentiments. And the man who is ostensibly contradicting me is merely expressing his moral sentiments. So that there is plainly no sense in asking which of us is in the right. For neither of us is asserting a genuine proposition.

What we have just been saying about the symbol "wrong" applies to all normative ethical symbols. Sometimes they occur in sentences which record ordinary empirical facts besides expressing ethical feeling about those facts: sometimes they occur in sentences which simply express ethical feeling about a certain type of action, or situation, without making any statement of fact. But in every case in which one would commonly be said to be making an ethical judgement, the function of the relevant ethical word is purely "emotive." It is used to express feeling about certain objects, but not to make any assertion about them.

It is worth mentioning that ethical terms do not serve only to express feeling. They are calculated also to arouse feeling, and so to stimulate action. Indeed some of them are used in such a way as to give the sentences in which they occur the effect of commands. Thus the sentence "It is your duty to tell the truth" may be regarded both as the expression of a certain sort of ethical feeling about truthfulness and as the expression of the command "Tell the truth." The sentence "You ought to tell the truth" also involves the command "Tell the truth," but here the tone of the command is less emphatic. In the sentence "It is good to tell the truth" the command has become little more than a suggestion. And thus the "meaning" of the word "good," in its ethical usage, is differentiated from that of the word "duty" or the word "ought." In fact we may define the meaning of the various ethical words in terms both of the different feelings they are ordinarily taken to express, and also the different responses which they are calculated to provoke.

We can now see why it is impossible to find a criterion for determining the validity of ethical judgements. It is not because they have an "absolute" validity which is mysteriously independent of ordinary sense-experience, but because they have no objective validity whatsoever. If a sentence makes no statement at all, there is obviously no sense in asking whether what it says is true or false. And we have seen that sentences which simply express moral judgements do not say anything. They are pure expressions of feeling and as such do not come under the category of truth and falsehood. They are unverifiable for the same reason

108

as a cry of pain or a word of command is unverifiable—because they do not express genuine propositions.

Thus, although our theory of ethics might fairly be said to be radically subjectivist, it differs in a very important respect from the orthodox subjectivist theory. For the orthodox subjectivist does not deny, as we do, that the sentences of a moralizer express genuine propositions. All he denies is that they express propositions of a unique non-empirical character. His own view is that they express propositions about the speaker's feelings. If this were so, ethical judgements clearly would be capable of being true or false. They would be true if the speaker had the relevant feelings, and false if he had not. And this is a matter which is, in principle, empirically verifiable. Furthermore they could be significantly contradicted. For if I say, "Tolerance is a virtue," and someone answers, "You don't approve of it," he would, on the ordinary subjectivist theory, be contradicting me. On our theory, he would not be contradicting me, because, in saying that tolerance was a virtue, I should not be making any statement about my own feelings or about anything else. I should simply be evincing my feelings, which is not at all the same thing as saying that I have them.

The distinction between the expression of feeling and the assertion of feeling is complicated by the fact that the assertion that one has a certain feeling often accompanies the expression of that feeling, and is then, indeed, a factor in the expression of that feeling. Thus I may simultaneously express boredom and say that I am bored, and in that case my utterance of the words, "I am bored," is one of the circumstances which make it true to say that I am expressing or evincing boredom. But I can express boredom without actually saying that I am bored. I can express it by my tone and gestures, while making a statement about something wholly unconnected with it, or by an ejaculation, or without uttering any words at all. So that even if the assertion that one has a certain feeling always involves the expression of that feeling, the expression of a feeling assuredly does not always involve the assertion that one has it. And this is the important point to grasp in considering the distinction between our theory and the ordinary subjectivist theory. For whereas the subjectivist holds that ethical statements actually assert the existence of certain feelings, we hold that ethical statements are expressions and excitants of feeling which do not necessarily involve any assertions.

We have already remarked that the main objection to the ordinary subjectivist theory is that the validity of ethical judgements is not determined by the nature of their author's feelings. And this is an objection which our theory escapes. For it does not imply that the existence of any feelings is a necessary and sufficient condition of the validity of an ethical judgement. It implies, on the contrary, that ethical judgements have no validity.

There is, however, a celebrated argument against subjectivist theories which our theory does not escape. It has been pointed out by Moore that if ethical statements were simply statements about the speaker's feelings, it would be impossible to argue about questions of value.[1] To take a typical example: if a man said that thrift was a virtue, and another replied that it was a vice, they would not, on this theory, be disputing with one another. One would be saying that he approved of thrift, and the other that *he* didn't; and there is no reason why both these statements should not be true. Now Moore held it to be obvious that we do dispute about questions of value, and accordingly concluded that the particular form of subjectivism which he was discussing was false.

It is plain that the conclusion that it is impossible to dispute about questions of value follows from our theory also. For as we hold that such sentences as "Thrift is a virtue" and "Thrift is a vice" do not express propositions at all, we clearly cannot hold that they express incompatible propositions. We must therefore admit that if Moore's argument really refutes the ordinary subjectivist theory, it also refutes ours. But, in fact, we deny that it does refute even the ordinary subjectivist theory. For we hold that one really never does dispute about questions of value.

This may seem, at first sight, to be a very paradoxical assertion. For we certainly do engage in disputes which are ordinarily regarded as disputes about questions of value. But, in all such cases, we find, if we consider the matter closely, that the dispute is not really about a question of value, but about a question of fact. When someone disagrees with us about the moral value of a certain action or type of action, we do admittedly resort to argument in order to win him over to our way of thinking. But we do

[1] cf. *Philosophical Studies*, "The Nature of Moral Philosophy."

not attempt to show by our arguments that he has the "wrong" ethical feeling towards a situation whose nature he has correctly apprehended. What we attempt to show is that he is mistaken about the facts of the case. We argue that he has misconceived the agent's motive: or that he has misjudged the effects of the action, or its probable effects in view of the agent's knowledge; or that he has failed to take into account the special circumstances in which the agent was placed. Or else we employ more general arguments about the effects which actions of a certain type tend to produce, or the qualities which are usually manifested in their performance. We do this in the hope that we have only to get our opponent to agree with us about the nature of the empirical facts for him to adopt the same moral attitude towards them as we do. And as the people with whom we argue have generally received the same moral education as ourselves, and live in the same social order, our expectation is usually justified. But if our opponent happens to have undergone a different process of moral "conditioning" from ourselves, so that, even when he acknowledges all the facts, he still disagrees with us about the moral value of the actions under discussion, then we abandon the attempt to convince him by argument. We say that it is impossible to argue with him because he has a distorted or undeveloped moral sense; which signifies merely that he employs a different set of values from our own. We feel that our own system of values is superior, and therefore speak in such derogatory terms of his. But we cannot bring forward any arguments to show that our system is superior. For our judgement that it is so is itself a judgement of value, and accordingly outside the scope of argument. It is because argument fails us when we come to deal with pure questions of value, as distinct from questions of fact, that we finally resort to mere abuse.

In short, we find that argument is possible on moral questions only if some system of values is presupposed. If our opponent concurs with us in expressing moral disapproval of all actions of a given type t, then we may get him to condemn a particular action A, by bringing forward arguments to show that A is of type t. For the question whether A does or does not belong to that type is a plain question of fact. Given that a man has certain moral principles, we argue that he must, in order to be consistent, react morally to certain things in a certain way. What we do not and cannot argue about is the validity of these moral principles. We merely praise or condemn them in the light of our own feelings.

If anyone doubts the accuracy of this account of moral disputes, let him try to construct even an imaginary argument on a question of value which does not reduce itself to an argument about a question of logic or about an empirical matter of fact. I am confident that he will not succeed in producing a single example. And if that is the case, he must allow that its involving the impossibility of purely ethical arguments is not, as Moore thought, a ground of objection to our theory, but rather a point in favour of it.

Having upheld our theory against the only criticism which appeared to threaten it, we may now use it to define the nature of all ethical enquiries. We find that ethical philosophy consists simply in saying that ethical concepts are pseudo-concepts and therefore unanalysable. The further task of describing the different feelings that the different ethical terms are used to express, and the different reactions that they customarily provoke, is a task for the psychologist. There cannot be such a thing as ethical science, if by ethical science one means the elaboration of a "true" system of morals. For we have seen that, as ethical judgements are mere expressions of feeling, there can be no way of determining the validity of any ethical system, and, indeed, no sense in asking whether any such system is true. All that one may legitimately enquire in this connection is, What are the moral habits of a given person or group of people, and what causes them to have precisely those habits and feelings? And this enquiry falls wholly within the scope of the existing social sciences.

It appears, then, that ethics, as a branch of knowledge, is nothing more than a department of psychology and sociology. And in case anyone thinks that we are overlooking the existence of casuistry, we may remark that casuistry is not a science, but is a purely analytical investigation of the structure of a given moral system. In other words, it is an exercise in formal logic.

When one comes to pursue the psychological enquiries which constitute ethical science, one is immediately enabled to account for the Kantian and hedonistic theories of morals. For one finds that one of the chief causes of moral behaviour is fear, both conscious and unconscious, of a god's displeasure, and fear of the enmity of society. And this, indeed, is the reason why moral precepts present themselves to some people as "categorical" commands. And one finds, also, that the moral code of a society is partly determined by the beliefs of that society concerning the conditions of its own happiness—or, in other words, that a society tends to encourage or discourage a given type of conduct by the use of moral sanctions according as it appears to promote or detract from the contentment of the society as a whole. And this is the reason why altruism is recommended in most moral codes and egotism condemned. It is from the observation of this connection between morality and happiness that hedonistic or eudæmonistic theories of morals ultimately spring, just as the moral theory of Kant is based on the fact, previously explained, that moral precepts have for some people the force of inexorable commands. As each of these theories ignores the fact which lies at the root of the other, both may be criticized as being one-sided; but this is not the main objection to either of them. Their essential defect is that they treat propositions which refer to the causes and attributes of our ethical feelings as if they were definitions of ethical concepts. And thus they fail to recognise that ethical concepts are pseudo-concepts and consequently indefinable.

As we have already said, our conclusions about the nature of ethics apply to æsthetics also. Æsthetic terms are used in exactly the same way as ethical terms. Such æsthetic words as "beautiful" and "hideous" are employed, as ethical words are employed, not to make statements of fact, but simply to express certain feelings and evoke a certain response. It follows, as in ethics, that there is no sense in attributing objective validity to æsthetic judgements, and no possibility of arguing about questions of value in æsthetics, but only about questions of fact. A scientific treatment of æsthetics would show us what in general were the causes of æsthetic feeling, why various societies produced and admired the works of art they did, why taste varies as it does within a given society, and so forth. And these are ordinary psychological or sociological questions. They have, of course, little or nothing to do with æsthetic criticism as we understand it. But that is because the purpose of æsthetic criticism is not so much to give knowledge as to communicate emotion. The critic, by calling attention to certain features of the work under review, and expressing his own feelings about them, endeavours to make us share his attitude towards the work as a whole. The only relevant propositions that he formulates are propositions describing the nature of the work. And these are plain records of fact. We conclude, therefore, that there is nothing in æsthetics, any more than there is in ethics, to justify the view that it embodies a unique type of knowledge.

It should now be clear that the only information which we can legitimately derive from the study of our æsthetic and moral experiences is information about our own mental and physical make-up. We take note of these experiences as providing data for our psychological and sociological generalisations. And this is the only way in which they serve to increase our knowledge. It follows that any attempt to make our use of ethical and æsthetic concepts the basis of a metaphysical theory concerning the existence of a world of values, as distinct from the world of facts, involves a false analysis of these concepts. Our own analysis has shown that the phenomena of moral experience cannot fairly be used to support any rationalist or metaphysical doctrine whatsoever. In particular, they cannot, as Kant hoped, be used to establish the existence of a transcendent god.

This mention of God brings us to the question of the possibility of religious knowledge. We shall see that this possibility has already been ruled out by our treatment of metaphysics. But, as this is a point of considerable interest, we may be permitted to discuss it at some length.

It is now generally admitted, at any rate by philosophers, that the existence of a being having the attributes which define the god of any non-animistic religion cannot be demonstratively proved. To see that this is so, we have only to ask ourselves what are the premises from which the existence of such a god could be deduced. If the conclusion that a god exists is to be demonstratively certain, then these premises must be certain; for, as the conclusion of a deductive argument is already contained in the premises, any uncertainty there may be about the truth of the premises is necessarily shared by it. But we know that no empirical proposition can ever be anything more than probable. It is only *a priori* propositions that are logically certain. But we cannot deduce the existence of a god from an *a priori* proposition. For we know that the reason why *a priori* propositions are certain is that they are tautologies. And from a set of tautologies nothing but a further tautology can be validly deduced. It follows that there is no possibility of demonstrating the existence of a god.

What is not so generally recognised is that there can be no way of proving that the existence of a god, such as the God of Christianity, is even probable. Yet this also is easily shown. For if the existence of such a god were probable, then the proposition that he existed would be an empirical hypothesis. And in that case it would be possible to deduce from it, and other empirical hypotheses, certain experiential propositions which were not deducible from those other hypotheses alone. But in fact this is not possible. It is sometimes claimed, indeed, that the existence of a certain sort of regularity in nature constitutes sufficient evidence for the existence of a god. But if the sentence "God exists" entails no more than that certain types of phenomena occur in certain sequences, then to assert the existence of a god will be simply equivalent to asserting that there is the requisite regularity in nature; and no religious man would admit that this was all he intended to assert in asserting the existence of a god. He would say that in talking about God, he was talking about a transcendent being who might be known through certain empirical manifestations, but certainly could not be defined in terms of those manifestations. But in that case the term "god" is a metaphysical term. And if "god" is a metaphysical term, then it cannot be even probable that a god exists. For to say that "God exists" is to make a metaphysical utterance which cannot be either true or false. And by the same criterion, no sentence which purports to describe the nature of a transcendent god can possess any literal significance.

It is important not to confuse this view of religious assertions with the view that is adopted by atheists, or agnostics.[1] For it is characteristic of an agnostic to hold that the existence of a god is a possibility in which there is no good reason either to believe or disbelieve; and it is characteristic of an atheist to hold that it is at least probable that no god exists. And our view that all utterances about the nature of God are nonsensical, so far from being identical with, or even lending any support to, either of these familiar contentions, is actually incompatible with them. For if the assertion that there is a god is nonsensical, then the atheist's assertion that there is no god is equally nonsensical, since it is only a significant proposition that can be significantly contradicted. As for the

[1] This point was suggested to me by Professor H. H. Price.

agnostic, although he refrains from saying either that there is or that there is not a god, he does not deny that the question whether a transcendent god exists is a genuine question. He does not deny that the two sentences "There is a transcendent god" and "There is no transcendent god" express propositions one of which is actually true and the other false. All he says is that we have no means of telling which of them is true, and therefore ought not to commit ourselves to either. But we have seen that the sentences in question do not express propositions at all. And this means that agnosticism also is ruled out.

Thus we offer the theist the same comfort as we gave to the moralist. His assertions cannot possibly be valid, but they cannot be invalid either. As he says nothing at all about the world, he cannot justly be accused of saying anything false, or anything for which he has insufficient grounds. It is only when the theist claims that in asserting the existence of a transcendent god he is expressing a genuine proposition that we are entitled to disagree with him.

It is to be remarked that in cases where deities are identified with natural objects, assertions concerning them may be allowed to be significant. If, for example, a man tells me that the occurrence of thunder is alone both necessary and sufficient to establish the truth of the proposition that Jehovah is angry, I may conclude that, in his usage of words, the sentence "Jehovah is angry" is equivalent to "It is thundering." But in sophisticated religions, though they may be to some extent based on men's awe of natural process which they cannot sufficiently understand, the "person" who is supposed to control the empirical world is not himself located in it; he is held to be superior to the empirical world, and so outside it; and he is endowed with super-empirical attributes. But the notion of a person whose essential attributes are non-empirical is not an intelligible notion at all. We may have a word which is used as if it named this "person," but, unless the sentences in which it occurs express propositions which are empirically verifiable, it cannot be said to symbolize anything. And this is the case with regard to the word "god," in the usage in which it is intended to refer to a transcendent object. The mere existence of the noun is enough to foster the illusion that there is a real, or at any rate a possible entity corresponding to it. It is only when we enquire what God's attributes are that we discover that "God," in this usage, is not a genuine name.

It is common to find belief in a transcendent god conjoined with belief in an after-life. But, in the form which it usually takes, the content of this belief is not a genuine hypothesis. To say that men do not ever die, or that the state of death is merely a state of prolonged insensibility, is indeed to express a significant proposition, though all the available evidence goes to show that it is false. But to say that there is something imperceptible inside a man, which is his soul or his real self, and that it goes on living after he is dead, is to make a metaphysical assertion which has no more factual content than the assertion that there is a transcendent god.

It is worth mentioning that, according to the account which we have given of religious assertions, there is no logical ground for antagonism between religion and natural science. As far as the question of truth or falsehood is concerned, there is no opposition between the natural scientist and the theist who believes in a transcendent god. For since the religious utterances of the theist are not genuine propositions at all, they cannot stand in any logical relation to the propositions of science. Such antagonism as there is between religion and science appears to consist in the fact that science takes away one of the motives which make men religious. For it is acknowledged that one of the ultimate sources of religious feeling lies in the inability of men to determine their own destiny; and science tends to destroy the feeling of awe with which men regard an alien world, by making them believe that they can understand and anticipate the course of natural phenomena, and even to some extent control it. The fact that it has recently become fashionable for physicists themselves to be sympathetic towards religion is a point in favour of this hypothesis. For this sympathy towards religion marks the physicists' own lack of confidence in the validity of their hypotheses, which is a reaction on their part from the anti-religious dogmatism of nineteenth-century scientists, and a natural outcome of the crisis through which physics has just passed.

It is not within the scope of this enquiry to enter more deeply into the causes of religious feeling, or to discuss the probability of the continuance of religious belief. We are concerned only to answer those questions which arise out of our discussion of the possibility of religious knowledge. The point which we wish to establish is that there cannot be any transcendent truths of religion. For the sentences which the theist uses to express such "truths" are not literally significant.

An interesting feature of this conclusion is that it accords with what many theists are accustomed to say themselves. For we are often told that the nature of God is a mystery which transcends the human understanding. But to say that something transcends the human understanding is to say that it is unintelligible. And what is unintelligible cannot significantly be described. Again, we are told that God is not an object of reason but an object of faith. This may be nothing more than an admission that the existence of God must be taken on trust, since it cannot be proved. But it may also be an assertion that God is the object of a purely mystical intuition, and cannot therefore be defined in terms which are intelligible to the reason. And I think there are many theists who would assert this. But if one allows that it is impossible to define God in intelligible terms, then one is allowing that it is impossible for a sentence both to be significant and to be about God. If a mystic admits that the object of his vision is something which cannot be described, then he must also admit that he is bound to talk nonsense when he describes it.

For his part, the mystic may protest that his intuition does reveal truths to him, even though he cannot explain to others what these truths are; and that we who do not possess this faculty of intuition can have no ground for denying that it is a cognitive faculty. For we can hardly maintain *a priori* that there are no ways of discovering true propositions except those which we ourselves employ. The answer is that we set no limit to the number of ways in which one may come to formulate a true proposition. We do not in any way deny that a synthetic truth may be discovered by purely intuitive methods as well as by the rational method of induction. But we do say that every synthetic proposition, however it may have been arrived at, must be subject to the test of actual experience. We do not deny *a priori* that the mystic is able to discover truths by his own special methods. We wait to hear what are the propositions which embody his discoveries, in order to see whether they are verified or confuted by our empirical observations. But the mystic, so far from producing propositions which are empirically verified, is unable to produce any intelligible propositions at all. And therefore we say that his intuition has not revealed to him any facts. It is no use his saying that he has apprehended facts but is unable to express them. For we know that if he really had acquired any information, he would be able to express it. He would be able to indicate in some way or other how the genuineness of his discovery might be empirically determined. The fact that he cannot reveal what he "knows," or even himself devise an empirical test to validate his "knowledge," shows that his state of mystical intuition is not a genuinely cognitive state. So that in describing his vision the mystic does not give us any information about the external world; he merely gives us indirect information about the condition of his own mind.

These considerations dispose of the argument from religious experience, which many philosophers still regard as a valid argument in favour of the existence of a god. They say that it is logically possible for men to be immediately acquainted with God, as they are immediately acquainted with a sense-content, and that there is no reason why one should be prepared to believe a man when he says that he is seeing a yellow patch, and refuse to believe him when he says that he is seeing God. The answer to this is that if the man who asserts that he is seeing God is merely asserting that he is experiencing a peculiar kind of sense-content, then we do not for a moment deny that his assertion may be true. But, ordinarily, the man who says that he is seeing God is saying not merely that he is experiencing a religious emotion, but also that there exists a transcendent being who is the object of this emotion; just as the man who says that he sees a yellow patch is ordinarily saying not merely that his visual sense-field contains a yellow sense-content, but also that there exists a yellow object to which the sense-content belongs. And it is not irrational to be prepared to believe a man when he asserts the existence of a yellow object, and to refuse to believe him when he asserts the existence of a transcendent god. For whereas the sentence "There exists here a yellow-coloured material thing" expresses a genuine synthetic proposition which could be empirically verified, the sentence "There exists a transcendent god" has, as we have seen, no literal significance.

We conclude, therefore, that the argument from religious experience is altogether fallacious. The fact that people have religious experiences is interesting from the psychological point of view, but it does not in any way imply that there is such a thing as religious knowledge, any more than our having moral experiences implies that there is such a thing as moral knowledge. The theist, like the moralist, may believe that his experiences are cognitive experiences, but, unless he can formulate his "knowledge" in propositions that are empirically verifiable, we may be sure that he is deceiving himself. It follows that those philosophers who fill their books with assertions that they intuitively "know" this or that moral or religious "truth" are merely providing material for the psycho-analyst. For no act of intuition can be said to reveal a truth about any matter of fact unless it issues in verifiable propositions. And all such propositions are to be incorporated in the system of empirical propositions which constitutes science.

CHAPTER VII

THE SELF AND THE COMMON WORLD

It is customary for the authors of epistemological treatises to assume that our empirical knowledge must have a basis of certainty, and that there must therefore be objects whose existence is logically indubitable. And they believe, for the most part, that it is their business, not merely to describe these objects, which they regard as being immediately "given" to us, but also to provide a logical proof of the existence of objects which are not so "given." For they think that without such a proof the greater part of our so-called empirical knowledge will lack the certification which it logically requires.

To those who have followed the argument of this book it will, however, be clear that these familiar assumptions are mistaken. For we have seen that our claims to empirical knowledge are not susceptible of a logical, but only of a pragmatic, justification. It is futile, and therefore illegitimate, to demand an *a priori* proof of the existence of objects which are not immediately "given." For, unless they are metaphysical objects, the occurrence of certain sense-experiences will itself constitute the only proof of their existence which is requisite or obtainable; and the question whether the appropriate sense-experiences do or do not occur in the relevant circumstances is one that must be decided in actual practice, and not by any *a priori* argumentation. We have already applied these considerations to the so-called problem of perception, and we shall shortly be applying them also to the traditional "problems" of our knowledge of our own existence, and of the existence of other people. In the case of the problem of perception, we found that in order to avoid metaphysics we were obliged to adopt a phenomenalist standpoint, and we shall find that the same treatment must be accorded to the other problems to which we have just now referred.

We have seen, furthermore, that there are no objects whose existence is indubitable. For, since existence is not a predicate, to assert that an object exists is always to assert a synthetic proposition; and it has been shown that no synthetic propositions are logically sacrosanct. All of them, including the propositions which describe the content of our sensations, are hypotheses which, however great their probability, we may eventually find it expedient to abandon. And this means that our empirical knowledge cannot have a basis of logical certainty. It follows, indeed, from the definition of a synthetic proposition that it cannot be either proved or disproved by formal logic. The man who denies such a proposition may be acting irrationally, by contemporary standards of rationality, but he is not necessarily contradicting himself. And we know that the only propositions that are certain are those which cannot be denied without self-contradiction, inasmuch as they are tautologies.

It must not be thought that in denying that our empirical knowledge has a basis of certainty we are denying that any objects are really "given." For to say that an object is immediately "given" is to say merely that it is the content of a sense-experience, and we are very far from maintaining that our sense-experiences have no real content, or even that their content is in any way indescribable. All that we are maintaining in this connection is that any description of the content of any sense-experience is an empirical hypothesis of whose validity there can be no guarantee. And this is by no means equivalent to maintaining that no such hypothesis can actually be valid. We shall not, indeed, attempt to formulate any such hypotheses ourselves, because the discussion of psychological questions is out of place in a philosophical enquiry; and we have already made it clear that our empiricism is not logically dependent on an atomistic psychology, such as Hume and Mach adopted, but is compatible with any theory whatsoever concerning the actual characteristics of our sensory fields. For the empiricist doctrine to which we are committed is a logical doctrine concerning the distinction between analytic propositions, synthetic propositions, and metaphysical verbiage; and as such it has no bearing on any psychological question of fact.

It is not possible, however, to set aside all the questions which philosophers have raised in connection with the "given" as being psychological in character, and so outside the scope of this enquiry. In particular, it is impossible to deal in this way with the question whether sense-contents are mental or physical, or with the question whether they are in any sense private to a single self, or with the question whether they can exist without being experienced. For none of these three questions is capable of being solved by an empirical test. They must, if they are soluble at all, be soluble *a priori*. And as they are all questions which have given rise to much dispute among philosophers, we shall in fact attempt to provide for each of them a definitive *a priori* solution.

To begin with, we must make it clear that we do not accept the realist analysis of our sensations in terms of subject, act, and object. For neither the existence of the substance which is supposed to perform the so-called act of sensing nor the existence of the act itself, as an entity distinct from the sense-contents on which it is supposed to be directed, is in the least capable of being verified. We do not deny, indeed, that a given sense-content can legitimately be said to be experienced by a particular subject; but we shall see that this relation of being experienced by a particular subject is to be analysed in terms of the relationship of sense-contents to one another, and not in terms of a substantival ego and its mysterious acts. Accordingly we define a sense-content not as the object, but as a part of a sense-experience. And from this it follows that the existence of a sense-content always entails the existence of a sense-experience.

It is necessary, at this point, to remark that when one says that a sense-experience, or a sense-content, exists, one is making a different type of statement from that which one makes when one says that a material thing exists. For the existence of a material thing is defined in terms of the actual and possible occurrence of the sense-contents which constitute it as a logical construction, and one cannot significantly speak of a sense-experience, which is a whole composed of sense-contents, or of a sense-content itself as if it were a logical construction out of sense-contents. And in fact when we say that a given sense-content or sense-experience exists, we are saying no more than that it occurs. And, accordingly, it seems advisable always to speak of the "occurrence" of sense-contents and sense-experiences in preference to speaking of their "existence," and so to avoid the danger of treating sense-contents as if they were material things.

The answer to the question whether sense-contents are mental or physical is that they are neither; or rather, that the distinction between what is mental and what is physical does not apply to sense-contents. It applies only to objects which are logical constructions out of them. But what differentiates one such logical construction from another is the fact that it is constituted by different sense-contents or by sense-contents differently related. So that when we distinguish a given mental object from a given physical object, or a mental object from another mental object, or a physical object from another physical object, we are in every case distinguishing between different logical constructions whose elements cannot themselves be said to be either mental or physical. It is, indeed, not impossible for a sense-content to be an element both of a mental and of a physical object; but it is necessary that some of the elements, or some of the relations, should be different in the two logical constructions. And it may be advisable here to repeat that, when we refer to an object as a logical construction out of certain sense-contents, we are not saying that it is actually constructed out of those sense-contents, or that the sense-contents are in any way parts of it, but are merely expressing, in a convenient, if somewhat misleading, fashion, the syntactical fact that all sentences referring to it are translatable into sentences referring to them.

The fact that the distinction between mind and matter applies only to logical constructions and that all distinctions between logical constructions are reducible to distinctions between sense-contents, proves that the difference between the entire class of mental objects and the entire class of physical objects is not in any sense more fundamental than the difference between any two sub-classes of mental objects, or the difference between any two sub-classes of physical objects. Actually, the distinguishing feature of the objects belonging to the category of "one's own mental states" is the fact that they are mainly constituted by "introspective" sense-contents and by sense-contents which are elements of one's own body; and the distinguishing feature of the objects belonging to the category of "the mental states of others" is the fact that they are mainly constituted by sense-contents which are elements of other living bodies; and what makes one unite these two classes of objects to form the single class of mental objects is the fact that there is a high degree of qualitative similarity between many of the sense-contents which are elements of other living bodies and many of the elements of one's own. But we are not now concerned with the provision of an exact definition of "mentality." We are interested only in making it plain that the distinction between mind and matter, applying as it does to logical constructions out of sense-contents, cannot apply to sense-contents themselves. For a distinction between logical constructions which is constituted by the fact that there are certain distinctions between their elements is clearly of a different type from any distinction that can obtain between the elements.

It should be clear, also, that there is no philosophical problem concerning the relationship of mind and matter, other than the linguistic problems of defining certain symbols which denote logical constructions in terms of symbols which denote sense-contents. The problems with which philosophers have vexed themselves in the past, concerning the possibility of bridging the "gulf" between mind and matter in knowledge or in action, are all fictitious problems arising out of the senseless metaphysical conception of mind and matter, or minds and material things, as "substances." Being freed from metaphysics, we see that there can be no *a priori* objections to the existence either of causal or of epistemological connections between minds and material things. For, roughly speaking, all that we are saying when we say that the mental state of a person A at a time t is a state of awareness of a material thing X, is that the sense-experience which is the element of A occurring at time t contains a sense-content which is an element of X, and also certain images which define A's expectation of the occurrence in suitable circumstances of certain further elements of X, and that this expectation is correct: and what we are saying when we assert that a mental object M and a physical object X are causally connected is that, in certain conditions, the occurrence of a certain sort of sense-content, which is an element of M, is a reliable sign of the occurrence of a certain sort of sense-content, which is an element of X, or vice versa, And the question whether any propositions of these kinds are true or not is clearly an empirical question. It cannot be decided, as metaphysicians have attempted to decide it, *a priori*.

We turn now to consider the question of the subjectivity of sense-contents—that is, to consider whether it is or is not logically possible for a sense-content to occur in the sense-history of more than a single self. And in order to decide this question we must proceed to give an analysis of the notion of a self.

The problem which now confronts us is analogous to the problem of perception with which we have already dealt. We know that a self, if it is not to be treated as a metaphysical entity, must be held to be a logical construction out of sense-experiences. It is, in fact, a logical construction out of the sense-experiences which constitute the actual and possible sense-history of a self. And, accordingly, if we ask what is the nature of the self, we are asking what is the relationship that must obtain between sense-experiences for them to belong to the sense-history of the same self. And the answer to this question is that for any two sense-experiences to belong to the sense-history of the same self it is necessary and sufficient that they should contain organic sense-contents which are elements of the same body.[1] But, as it is logically impossible for any organic sense-content to be an element of more than one body, the relation of "belonging to the sense-history of the same self" turns out to be a symmetrical and transitive relation.[2] And, from the fact that the relation of belonging to the sense-history of the same self is symmetrical and transitive, it follows necessarily that the series of sense-experiences which constitute the sense-histories of different selves cannot have any members in common. And this is tantamount to saying that it is logically impossible for a sense-experience to belong to the sense-history of more than a single self. But if all sense-experiences

[1] This is not the only criterion. Vide *The Foundations of Empirical Knowledge*, pp. 142–4.
[2] For a definition of a symmetrical transitive relation, see Chapter III, p. 66.

are subjective, then, all sense-contents are subjective. For it is necessary by definition for a sense-content to be contained in a single sense-experience.

To many people, the account of the self, on which this conclusion depends, will no doubt appear paradoxical. For it is still fashionable to regard the self as a substance. But, when one comes to enquire into the nature of this substance, one finds that it is an entirely unobservable entity. It may be suggested that it is revealed in self-consciousness but this is not the case. For all that is involved in self-consciousness is the ability of a self to remember some of its earlier states. And to say that a self A is able to remember some of its earlier states is to say merely that some of the sense-experiences which constitute A contain memory images which correspond to sense-contents which have previously occurred in the sense-history of A.[1] And thus we find that the possibility of self-consciousness in no way involves the existence of a substantive ego. But if the substantive ego is not revealed in self-consciousness, it is not revealed anywhere. The existence of such an entity is completely unverifiable. And accordingly, we must conclude that the assumption of its existence is no less metaphysical than Locke's discredited assumption of the existence of a material substratum. For it is clearly no more significant to assert that an "unobservable somewhat" underlies the sensations which are the sole empirical manifestations of the self than it is to assert that an "unobservable somewhat" underlies the sensations which are the sole empirical manifestations of a material thing. The considerations which make it necessary, as Berkeley saw, to give a phenomenalist account of material things, make it necessary also, as Berkeley did not see, to give a phenomenalist account of the self.

Our reasoning on this point, as on so many others, is in conformity with Hume's. He, too, rejected the notion of a substantive ego on the ground that no such entity was observable. For, he said, whenever he entered most intimately into what he called himself, he always stumbled on some particular perception or other—of heat or cold, light or shade, love or hatred, pain or pleasure. He never could catch himself at any time without a perception, and never could observe anything but the perception. And this led him to assert that a self was "nothing but a bundle

1 cf. Bertrand Russell, *Analysis of Mind*, Lecture IX.

or collection of different perceptions."[1] But, having asserted this, he found himself unable to discover the principle on which innumerable distinct perceptions among which it was impossible to perceive any "real connection" were united to form a single self. He saw that the memory must be regarded not as producing, but rather as discovering, personal identity—or, in other words, that, whereas self-consciousness has to be defined in terms of memory, self-identity cannot be; for the number of my perceptions which I can remember at any time always falls far short of the number of those which have actually occurred in my history, and those which I cannot remember are no less constitutive of my self than those which I can. But having, on this ground, rejected the claim of memory to be the unifying principle of the self, Hume was obliged to confess that he did not know what was the connection between perceptions in virtue of which they formed a single self.[2] And this confession has often been taken by rationalist authors as evidence that it is impossible for a consistent empiricist to give a satisfactory account of the self.

For our part, we have shown that this charge against empiricism is unfounded. For we have solved Hume's problem by defining personal identity in terms of bodily identity, and bodily identity is to be defined in terms of the resemblance and continuity of sense-contents. And this procedure is justified by the fact that whereas it is permissible, in our language, to speak of a man as surviving a complete loss of memory, or a complete change of character, it is self-contradictory to speak of a man as surviving the annihilation of his body.[3] For that which is supposed to survive by those who look forward to a "life after death" is not the empirical self, but a metaphysical entity—the soul. And this metaphysical entity, concerning which no genuine hypothesis can be formulated, has no logical connection whatsoever with the self.

It must, however, be remarked that, although we have vindicated Hume's contention that it is necessary to give a phenomenalist account of the nature of the self, our actual definition of the self is not a mere restatement of his. For we do not hold, as he apparently did, that the self is an aggregate of sense-experiences,

[1] *Treatise of Human Nature*, Book I, Part IV, section vi.

[2] *Treatise of Human Nature*, Appendix.

[3] This is not true if one adopts a psychological criterion of personal identity.

or that the sense-experiences which constitute a particular self are in any sense parts of it. What we hold is that the self is reducible to sense-experiences, in the sense that to say anything about the self is always to say something about sense-experiences; and our definition of personal identity is intended to show how this reduction could be made.

In thus combining a thoroughgoing phenomenalism with the admission that all sense-experiences, and the sense-contents which form part of them, are private to a single self, we are pursuing a course to which the following objection is likely to be raised. It will be said that anyone who maintains both that all empirical knowledge resolves itself on analysis into knowledge of the relationships of sense-contents, and also that the whole of a man's sense-history is private to himself, is logically obliged to be a solipsist—that is, to hold that no other people besides himself exist, or at any rate that there is no good reason to suppose that any other people beside himself exist. For it follows from his premises, so it will be argued, that the sense-experiences of another person cannot possibly form part of his own experience, and consequently that he cannot have the slightest ground for believing in their occurrence; and, in that case, if people are nothing but logical constructions out of their sense-experiences, he cannot have the slightest ground for believing in the existence of any other people. And it will be said that even if such a solipsistic doctrine cannot be shown to be self-contradictory, it is nevertheless known to be false[1]

I propose to meet this objection, not by denying that solipsism is known to be false, but by denying that it is a necessary consequence of our epistemology. I am, indeed, prepared to admit that if the personality of others was something that I could not possibly observe, then I should have no reason to believe in the existence of anyone else. And in admitting this I am conceding a point which would not, I think, be conceded by the majority of those philosophers who hold, as we do, that a sense-content cannot belong to the sense-history of more than a single self. They would maintain, on the contrary, that, although one cannot in any sense observe the existence of other people, one can nevertheless infer their existence with a high degree of probability from one's own experiences. They would say that my observation

[1] cf. L. S. Stebbing, *Logical Positivism and Analysis.*

of a body whose behaviour resembled the behaviour of my own body entitled me to think it probable that that body was related to a self which I could not observe, in the same way as my body was related to my own observable self. And in saying this, they would be attempting to answer not the psychological question, What causes me to believe in the existence of other people? but the logical question, What good reason have I for believing in the existence of other people? So that their view cannot be refuted, as is sometimes supposed, by an argument which shows that infants come by their belief in the existence of other people intuitively, and not through a process of inference. For although my belief in a certain proposition may in fact be causally dependent on my apprehension of the evidence which makes the belie1 rational, it is not necessary that it should be. It is not self contradictory to say that beliefs for which there are rational grounds are frequently arrived at by irrational means.

The correct way to refute this view that I can use an argument from analogy, based on the fact that there is a perceptible resemblance between the behaviour of other bodies and that of my own, to justify a belief in the existence of other people whose experiences I could not conceivably observe, is to point out that no argument can render probable a completely unverifiable hypothesis. I can legitimately use an argument from analogy to establish the probable existence of an object which has never in fact manifested itself in my experience, provided that the object is such that it could conceivably be manifested in my experience. If this condition is not fulfilled, then, as far as I am concerned, the object is a metaphysical object, and the assertion that it exists and has certain properties is a metaphysical assertion. And, since a metaphysical assertion is senseless, no argument can possibly render it probable. But, on the view which we are discussing, I must regard other people as metaphysical objects; for it is assumed that their experiences are completely inaccessible to my observation.

The conclusion to be drawn from this is not that the existence of other people is for me a metaphysical, and so fictitious, hypothesis, but that the assumption that other people's experiences are completely inaccessible to my observation is false: just as the conclusion to be drawn from the fact that Locke's notion of a material substratum is metaphysical is not that all the assertions which we make about material things are nonsensical, but that Locke's analysis of the concept of a material thing is false. And just as I must define material things and my own self in terms of their empirical manifestations, so I must define other people in terms of their empirical manifestations—that is, in terms of the behaviour of their bodies, and ultimately in terms of sense-contents. The assumption that "behind" these sense-contents there are entities which are not even in principle accessible to my observation can have no more significance for me than the admittedly metaphysical assumption that such entities "underlie" the sense-contents which constitute material things for me, or my own self. And thus I find that I have as good a reason to believe in the existence of other people as I have to believe in the existence of material things. For in each case my hypothesis is verified by the occurrence in my sense-history of the appropriate series of sense-contents.[1]

It must not be thought that this reduction of other people's experiences to one's own in any way involves a denial of their reality. Each of us must define the experiences of the others in terms of what he can at least in principle observe, but this does not mean that each of us must regard all the others as so many robots. On the contrary, the distinction between a conscious man and an unconscious machine resolves itself into a distinction between different types of perceptible behaviour. The only ground I can have for asserting that an object which appears to be a conscious being is not really a conscious being, but only a dummy or a machine, is that it fails to satisfy one of the empirical tests by which the presence or absence of consciousness is determined. If I know that an object behaves in every way as a conscious being must, by definition, behave, then I know that it is really conscious. And this is an analytical proposition. For when I assert that an object is conscious I am asserting no more than that it would, in response to any conceivable test, exhibit the empirical manifestations of consciousness. I am not making a metaphysical postulate concerning the occurrence of events which I could not, even in principle, observe.

It appears, then, that the fact that a man's sense-experiences are

[1] cf. Rudolf Carnap, "Scheinprobleme in der Philosophie: das Fremd-psychische und der Realismusstreit," and "Psychologie in physikalische Sprache," *Erkenntnis*, Vol. III, 1932.

private to himself, inasmuch as each of them contains an organic sense-content which belongs to his body and to no other, is perfectly compatible with his having good reason to believe in the existence of other men. For, if he is to avoid metaphysics, he must define the existence of other men in terms of the actual and hypothetical occurrence of certain sense-contents, and then the fact that the requisite sense-contents do occur in his sense-history gives him a good reason for believing that there are other conscious beings besides himself. And thus we see that the philosophical problem of "our knowledge of other people" is not the insoluble, and, indeed, fictitious, problem of establishing by argument the existence of entities which are altogether unobservable, but is simply the problem of indicating the way in which a certain type of hypothesis is empirically verified.[1]

It must be made clear, finally, that our phenomenalism is compatible not merely with the fact that each of us has good reason to believe that there exist a number of conscious beings of the same kind as himself, but also with the fact that each of us has good reason to believe that these beings communicate with one another and with him, and inhabit a common world. For it might appear, at first sight, as if the view that all synthetic propositions ultimately referred to sense-contents, coupled with the view that no sense-content could belong to the sense-history of more than one person, implied that no one could have any good reason to believe that a synthetic proposition ever had the same literal meaning for any other person as it had for himself. That is, it might be thought that if each person's experiences were private to himself, no one could have good reason to believe that any other person's experiences were qualitatively the same as his own, and consequently that no one could have good reason to believe that the propositions which he understood, referring as they did to the contents of his own sense-experiences, were ever understood in the same way by anybody else.[2] But this reasoning would be fallacious. It does not follow from the fact that each man's experiences are private to himself that no one ever has good reason to believe that another man's experiences are qualitatively the

[1] This question is referred to in the Introduction, pp. 19–20.

[2] This argument is used by Professor L. S. Stebbing in her article on "Communication and Verification," *Supplementary Proceedings of the Aristotelian Society, 1934.*

same as his own. For we define the qualitative identity and difference of two people's sense-experiences in terms of the similarity and dissimilarity of their reactions to empirical tests. To determine, for instance, whether two people have the same colour sense we observe whether they classify all the colour expanses with which they are confronted in the same way; and, when we say that a man is colour-blind, what we are asserting is that he classifies certain colour expanses in a different way from that in which they would be classified by the majority of people. It may be objected that the fact that two people classify colour expanses in the same way proves only that their colour worlds have the same structure, and not that they have the same content; that it is possible for another man to assent to every proposition which I make about colours on the basis of entirely different colour sensations, although, since the difference is systematic, neither of us is ever in a position to detect it. But the answer to this is that each of us has to define the content of another man's sense-experiences in terms of what he can himself observe. If he regards the experiences of others as essentially unobservable entities, whose nature has somehow to be inferred from the subjects' perceptible behaviour, then, as we have seen, even the proposition that there are other conscious beings becomes for him a metaphysical hypothesis. Accordingly, it is a mistake to draw a distinction between the structure and the content of people's sensations—such as that the structure alone is accessible to the observation of others, the content inaccessible. For if the contents of other people's sensations really were inaccessible to my observation, then I could never say anything about them. But, in fact, I do make significant statements about them; and that is because I define them, and the relations between them, in terms of what I can myself observe.

In the same way, each of us has good reason to suppose that other people understand him, and that he understands them, because he observes that his utterances have the effect on their actions which he regards as appropriate, and that they also regard as appropriate the effect which their utterances have on his actions; and mutual understanding is defined in terms of such harmony of behaviour. And, since to assert that two people inhabit a common world is to assert that they are capable, at least in principle, of understanding one another, it follows that each of us, although his sense-experiences are private to himself, has good reason to believe that he and other conscious beings inhabit a common world. For each of us observes the behaviour, on the part of himself and others, which constitutes the requisite understanding. And there is nothing in our epistemology which involves a denial of this fact.

CHAPTER VIII

SOLUTIONS OF OUTSTANDING PHILOSOPHICAL DISPUTES

ONE OF THE MAIN OBJECTS of this treatise has been to show that there is nothing in the nature of philosophy to warrant the existence of conflicting philosophical parties or "schools." For it is only when the available evidence is insufficient to determine the probability of a proposition that a difference of opinion concerning it is justifiable. But with regard to the propositions of philosophy this can never be the case. For, as we have seen, the function of the philosopher is not to devise speculative theories which require to be validated in experience, but to elicit the consequences of our linguistic usages. That is to say, the questions with which philosophy is concerned are purely logical questions; and although people do in fact dispute about logical questions, such disputes are always unwarranted. For they involve either the denial of a proposition which is necessarily true, or the assertion of a proposition which is necessarily false. In all such cases, therefore, we may be sure that one party to the dispute has been guilty of a miscalculation which a sufficiently close scrutiny of the reasoning will enable us to detect. So that if the dispute is not immediately resolved, it is because the logical error of which one party is guilty is too subtle to be easily detected, and not because the question at issue is irresoluble on the available evidence.

Accordingly, we who are interested in the condition of philosophy can no longer acquiesce in the existence of party divisions among philosophers. For we know that if the questions about which the parties contend are logical in character, they can be definitively answered. And, if they are not logical, they must either be dismissed as metaphysical, or made the subject of an empirical enquiry. I propose, therefore, to examine in turn the three great issues concerning which philosophers have differed in the past, to sort out the problems of which these issues consist, and to provide for each problem a solution appropriate to its nature. It will be found that some of these problems have already been dealt with in the course of this book, and in such cases we shall be content to recapitulate our solution without repeating the argument on which it was founded.

The questions which we are now about to consider are those that lie at issue between rationalists and empiricists, between realists and idealists, and between monists and pluralists. In each case, we shall find that the thesis which is maintained by one school and controverted by another is partly logical, partly metaphysical, and partly empirical, and that there is no strict logical connection between its constituent parts; so that it is legitimate to accept some portions of it and reject others. And, indeed, we do not claim that for anyone to be accounted a member of a particular school it is necessary for him to adhere to all the doctrines which we hold to be characteristic of the school, but rather that it is sufficient if he adheres to any of them. It is advisable for us to say this in order to protect ourselves against a possible charge of historical inaccuracy. But it must be understood from the outset that we are not concerned to vindicate any one set of philosophers at the expense of any other, but simply to settle certain questions which have played a part in the history of philosophy which is out of all proportion to their difficulty or their importance. We shall now begin with the questions which enter into the rationalist-empiricist controversy.

The metaphysical doctrine which is upheld by rationalists, and rejected by empiricists, is that there exists a supra-sensible world which is the object of a purely intellectual intuition and is alone wholly real. We have already dealt with this doctrine explicitly in the course of our attack on metaphysics, and seen that it is not even false but senseless. For no empirical observation could have the slightest tendency to establish any conclusion concerning the properties, or even the existence, of a supra-sensible world. And therefore we are entitled to deny the possibility of such a world and to dismiss as nonsensical the descriptions which have been given of it.

With the logical aspect of the rationalist-empiricist controversy we have also dealt very fully, and pronounced, it will be remembered, in favour of the empiricists. For we showed that a proposition only had factual content if it was empirically verifiable, and, consequently, that the rationalists were mistaken in supposing that there could be *a priori* propositions which referred to matters of fact. At the same time we disagreed with those empiricists who maintain that the distinction which is ordinarily drawn between *a priori* propositions and empirical propositions is an illegitimate distinction, and that all significant propositions are empirical hypotheses, whose truth may be in the highest degree probable but can never be certain. We admitted that there were propositions which were necessarily valid apart from all experience, and that there was a difference in kind between these propositions and empirical hypotheses. But we did not account for their necessity by saying, as a rationalist might, that they were speculative "truths of reason." We accounted for it by saying that they were tautologies. And we showed that the fact that we sometimes make mistakes in our *a priori* reasonings, and that even when we have not made any mistake we may arrive at an interesting and unexpected conclusion, is in no way incompatible with the fact that such reasonings are purely analytic. And thus we found that our rejection of the logical thesis of rationalism, and of all forms of metaphysics, did not oblige us to deny that there could be necessary truths.

An explicit rejection of metaphysics, as distinct from a mere abstention from metaphysical utterances, is characteristic of the type of empiricism which is known as positivism. But we have found ourselves unable to accept the criterion which the positivists employ to distinguish a metaphysical utterance from a genuine synthetic proposition. For they require of a synthetic proposition that it should, in principle at least, be conclusively verifiable. And as, for reasons which we have already given, no proposition is capable, even in principle, of being verified conclusively, but only at best of being rendered highly probable, the positivist criterion, so far from marking the distinction between literal sense and nonsense, as it is intended to do, makes every utterance nonsensical. And therefore, as we have seen, it is necessary to adopt a weakened form of the positivist verification principle, as a criterion of literal significance, and to allow a proposition to be genuinely factual if any empirical observations would be relevant to its truth or falsehood. So that an utterance is by us accounted metaphysical only if it is neither a tautology nor yet capable of being substantiated to any degree whatsoever by any possible observation. In practice, indeed, very little of what is allowed to be significant by this criterion would not be allowed also by the positivists. But that is because they do not apply their own criterion consistently.

It should be added that we dissent also from the positivist doctrine with regard to the significance of particular symbols. For it is characteristic of a positivist to hold that all symbols, other than logical constants, must either themselves stand for sense-contents or else be explicitly definable in terms of symbols which stand for sense-contents. It is plain that such physical symbols as "atom" or "molecule" or "electron" fail to satisfy this condition, and some positivists, including Mach, have been prepared on this account to regard the use of them as illegitimate.[1] They would not have been so ruthless if they had realised that they ought also, if they were to be consistent in the application of their criterion, to have condemned the use of symbols which stand for material things. For, as we have seen, even such familiar symbols as "table" or "chair" or "coat" cannot be defined explicitly in terms of symbols which stand for sense-contents, but only in use. And, accordingly, we must allow that the employment of a symbol is legitimate if it is possible, at any rate in principle, to give a rule for translating the sentences in which it occurs into sentences which refer to sense-contents—or, in other words, if it is possible to indicate how the propositions which it helps to express may be empirically substantiated. And this condition is as well satisfied by the physical symbols which positivists have condemned as by the symbols which stand for familiar material things.

Finally, it must again be emphasized that we are not committed by our logical thesis to any of the factual doctrines which have

[1] See Hans Hahn, "Logik, Mathematik und Naturerkennen," *Einheitswissenschaft*, Heft II, for a discussion of this question.

been propounded by empiricist authors. We have, indeed, already expressed our dissent from the psychological atomism of Mach and Hume; and we may add that, although we agree in the main with Hume's epistemological views concerning the validity of general propositions of law, we do not accept his account of the way in which such propositions actually come to be formulated. We do not hold, as he apparently did, that every general hypothesis is, in fact, a generalization from a number of observed instances. We agree with the rationalists that the process by which scientific theories come into being is often deductive rather than inductive. The scientist does not formulate his laws only as the result of seeing them exemplified in particular cases. Sometimes he considers the possibility of the law before he is in possession of the evidence which justifies it. It "occurs" to him that a certain hypothesis or set of hypotheses may be true. He employs deductive reasoning to discover what he ought to experience in a given situation if the hypothesis is true; and if he makes the required observations, or has reason to believe that he could make them, he accepts the hypothesis. He does not, as Hume implied, passively wait for nature to instruct him; rather, as Kant saw, does he force nature to answer the questions which he puts to her. So that there is a sense in which the rationalists are right in asserting that the mind is active in knowledge. It is not true, indeed, that the validity of a proposition is ever logically dependent upon the mental attitude of anyone towards it, nor is it true that every physical fact is either logically or causally dependent upon a mental fact, nor yet that observation of a physical object necessarily causes any change in it, although it may in fact do so in some cases. But it is true that the activity of theorizing is, in its subjective aspect, a creative activity, and that the psychological theories of empiricists concerning "the origins of our knowledge" are vitiated by their failure to take this into account.

But while it must be recognised that scientific laws are often discovered through a process of intuition, this does not mean that they can be intuitively validated. As we have said many times already, it is essential to distinguish the psychological question, How does our knowledge originate? from the logical question, How is it certified as knowledge? Whatever may be the correct answers to these two questions, it is clear that they are logically independent of one another. And, accordingly, we can consistently allow that the psychological theories of rationalists concerning the part played by intuition in the acquisition of our knowledge are very probably true, while at the same time we reject as self-contradictory their logical thesis that there are synthetic propositions of whose validity we have an *a priori* guarantee.

Whereas the main points in the dispute between rationalists and empiricists, of which we have now finally disposed, have been referred to constantly throughout this book, comparatively little attention has yet been paid to the realist-idealist controversy, which, to the historian of modern philosophy at any rate, is almost equally important. All that we have done so far in connection with it is to rule out its metaphysical aspect, and to assert that the logical questions which it involves are questions concerning the analysis of existential propositions. We have seen that the dispute between idealists and realists becomes a metaphysical dispute when it is assumed that the question whether an object is real or ideal is an empirical question which cannot be settled by any possible observation. We showed that in the ordinary sense of the term "real," the sense in which "being real" is opposed to "being illusory," there were definite empirical tests for determining whether an object was real or not; but that those who, agreeing that an object was real in this sense, went on to dispute whether it had a completely undetectable property, which they called also the property of being real, or an equally undetectable property of being ideal, were debating an altogether fictitious question. And to this we need not now add anything further, but may proceed at once to consider the realist-idealist controversy in its logical aspect.

The logical doctrines which are maintained by idealists and controverted by realists are all concerned with the question, What is entailed by sentences of the form "x is real"? Thus, it is the contention of Berkeleyan idealists that the sentence "x is real" or "x exists," where x stands for a thing and not for a person, is equivalent to "x is perceived," so that it is self-contradictory to assert that anything exists unperceived; and they hold, furthermore, that "x is perceived" entails "x is mental," and so conclude that everything that exists is mental. Both these propositions are denied by realists, who maintain for their part that the concept of reality is unanalysable, so that there is no sentence referring to perceptions which is equivalent to the sentence "x is real." In fact, we shall find that the realists are right in what they deny, but wrong in what they affirm.

Briefly, the grounds on which Berkeley held that no material thing could exist unperceived were these. He maintained, first, that a thing was nothing more than the sum of its sensible qualities, and, secondly, that it was self-contradictory to assert that a sensible quality existed unsensed. And from these premises it does follow that a thing cannot without self-contradiction be said to exist unperceived. But since he recognized that the common-sense assumption that things did exist when no human being was perceiving them was certainly not self-contradictory, and, indeed, himself believed it to be true, Berkeley allowed that a thing might exist unperceived by any human being, inasmuch as it could still be perceived by God. And he appears to have regarded the fact that he was obliged to rely on the perceptions of God to bring his doctrine into harmony with the fact that things very probably do exist at times when no human being is perceiving them as constituting a proof of the existence of a personal god: whereas, in truth, what it proves is that there is an error in Berkeley's reasoning. For, since propositions which assert the existence of material things have an undisputed factual significance, it cannot be correct to analyse them in terms of such metaphysical entities as the perceptions of a transcendent god.

We must now consider exactly where the error in Berkeley's reasoning lies. It is customary for realists to deny his proposition that a sensible quality cannot possibly exist unsensed. Taking him, I think rightly, to be using the terms "sensible quality" and "idea of sensation," as we have been using the term "sense-content," to refer to an entity which is sensibly given, they assert that he makes a faulty analysis of sensation through failing to distinguish between the object sensed and the act of consciousness which is directed upon it, and that there is no contradiction involved in supposing that the object may exist independently of the act.[1] But I do not think that this criticism is just. For these acts of sensing, which realists reproach Berkeley for having ignored,

[1] Vide G. E. Moore, *Philosophical Studies*, "The Refutation of Idealism."

appear to me to be completely inaccessible to any observation. And I suggest that those who believe in them have been misled by the grammatical fact that the sentences which they use to describe their sensations contain a transitive verb, just as those who believe that the self is given in sensation are misled by the fact that the sentences which people use to describe their sensations contain a grammatical subject: while what those who claim to detect the presence of such acts of sensing in their visual and tactual experiences are, I think, really detecting is the fact that their visual and tactual sense-fields have the sensible property of depth.[1] And, therefore, although Berkeley made a psychological error in supposing that the succession of "ideas" which constituted a person's sense-history was sensibly discrete, I believe that he was right to regard these "ideas" as the contents rather than the objects of sensations, and consequently that he was justified in asserting that a "sensible quality" could not conceivably exist unsensed. Accordingly we may allow that his dictum, *"Esse est percipi,"* is true with regard to sense-contents, for to speak of the existence of sense-contents is, as we have seen, merely a misleading way of speaking of their occurrence, and a sense-content cannot without self-contradiction be said to occur except as part of a sense-experience.

But although it is a fact that a sense-content cannot by definition occur without being experienced, and that material things are constituted by sense-contents, it is a mistake to conclude, as Berkeley did, that a material thing cannot exist unperceived. And the mistake is due to his misconception of the relationship between material things and the sense-contents which constitute them. If a material thing were really the sum of its "sensible qualities"—that is to say, an aggregate of sense-contents, or even a whole composed of sense-contents—then it would follow from the definitions of a material thing and a sense-content that no thing could exist unperceived. But, in fact, we have seen that sense-contents are not in any way parts of the material things which they constitute; the sense in which a material thing is reducible to sense-contents is simply that it is a logical construction and they are its elements; and this, as we have previously made clear, is a linguistic proposition which states that to say

[1] This point is made also by Rudolf Carnap in *Der logische Aufbau der Welt*, section 65.

anything about it is always equivalent to saying something about them. Moreover the elements of any given material thing are not merely actual but also possible sense-contents—that is to say, the sentences referring to sense-contents, which are the translations of the sentences referring to a material thing, need not necessarily express categorical propositions; they may be hypothetical. And this explains how it is possible for a material thing to exist throughout a period when none of its elements are actually experienced: it is sufficient that they should be capable of being experienced—that is, that there should be a hypothetical fact to the effect that, if certain conditions were fulfilled, certain sense-contents, belonging to the thing in question, would be experienced. There is, indeed, no contradiction involved in asserting the existence of a material thing which is never actually perceived. For in asserting that the thing existed, one would be asserting only that certain sense-contents would occur if a particular set of conditions relating to the faculties and the position of an observer was fulfilled; and such a hypothetical proposition may very well be true, even though the relevant conditions never are fulfilled. And, as we shall show later on, we may in some cases not merely have to recognise the existence of an unperceived material thing as a logical possibility, but may actually possess good inductive grounds for believing in it.

This analysis of propositions asserting the existence of material things, which is in conformity with Mill's conception of a material thing as "a permanent possibility of sensation," enables us not merely to dispense with the perceptions of God, but also to allow that people can be said to exist in the same sense as material things. It is, I think, a serious defect in Berkeley's theory that it does not allow this. For, failing to give the phenomenalist account of the self which, as Hume saw, his empiricism demanded, he found himself unable either to hold that the existence of people consisted, like the existence of material things, in their being perceived, or to put forward any other analysis of it. We, on the contrary, maintain that a man must define his own existence, and the existence of other people, no less than that of material things, in terms of the hypothetical occurrence of sense-contents. And I think we have succeeded in proving the necessity of such a thoroughgoing phenomenalism, and in meeting the objections to which it seems at first sight to be exposed.

The proposition that whatever is perceived is necessarily mental, which forms the second stage in the argument of the Berkeleyan idealist, rests on the assumption that the immediate data of sense are necessarily mental, together with the assumption that a thing is literally the sum of its "sensible qualities." And these are both assumptions which we have rejected. We have seen that a thing is to be defined, not as a collection of sense-contents, but as a logical construction out of them. And we have seen that the terms "mental" and "physical" apply only to logical constructions, and not to the immediate data of sense themselves. Sense-contents themselves cannot significantly be said either to be or not to be mental. And while it is certainly significant to assert that all the things which we ordinarily take to be unconscious are really conscious, we shall find that this is a proposition which we have very good reason to disbelieve.

I think that the idealist view that what is immediately given in sense-experience must necessarily be mental derives historically from an error of Descartes. For he, believing that he could deduce his own existence from the existence of a mental entity, a thought, without assuming the existence of any physical entity, concluded that his mind was a substance which was wholly independent of anything physical; so that it could directly experience only what belonged to itself. We have already seen that the premise of this argument is false; and, in any case, the conclusion does not follow from it. For, in the first place, the assertion that the mind is a substance, being a metaphysical assertion, cannot follow from anything. Secondly, if the term "thought" is used, as Descartes apparently used it, to refer to a single introspective sense-content, then a thought cannot, as in the ordinary usage, properly be said to be mental. And, finally, even if it were true that the existence of a conscious being could be validly deduced from an isolated mental datum, it would not in the least follow that such a being could not, in fact, stand in direct causal and epistemological relations to material things. And, indeed, we have previously shown that the proposition that mind and matter are completely independent is one which we have good empirical grounds for disbelieving, and one which no *a priori* argument could possibly serve to prove.

Although the responsibility for the view that it is possible to experience directly only what is mental rests ultimately with

Descartes, subsequent philosophers have supported it with arguments of their own. One of these is the so-called argument from illusion. This argument proceeds from the fact that the sensible appearances of a material thing vary with the point of view of the observer, or with his physical and psychological condition, or with the nature of the attendant circumstances such as the presence or absence of light. Each of these appearances is, it is argued, in itself as "good" as any other, but, since they are in many cases mutually incompatible, they cannot all really characterize the material thing; and thence it is concluded that none of them are "in the thing," but that they are all "in the mind." But this conclusion is plainly unwarranted. All that this argument from illusion proves is that the relationship of a sense-content to the material thing to which it belongs is not that of part to whole. It does not have the least tendency to show that any sense-content is "in the mind." Nor does the fact that a sense-content is partly dependent for its quality on the psychological state of an observer in any way go to prove that it is a mental entity itself.

Another argument of Berkeley's is superficially more plausible. He points out that sensations of all kinds are in some degree pleasant or painful, and argues that, as the sensation is not phenomenally distinguishable from the pleasure or the pain, the two must be identified. But pleasure and pain, he thinks, are indubitably mental, and so he concludes that the objects of sense are mental.[1] The error in this argument consists in the identification of pleasures and pains with particular sense-contents. It is true that the word "pain" is sometimes used to denote an organic sense-content, as in the sentence, "I feel a pain in my shoulder," but in this usage a pain cannot properly be said to be mental; and it is noteworthy that there is no corresponding usage of the word "pleasure." And in the usage in which pains and pleasures can properly be said to be mental, as in the sentence, "Domitian took pleasure in torturing flies," the terms denote, not sense-contents, but logical constructions. For to refer to pains and pleasures, in this usage, is a way of referring to people's behaviour, and so ultimately to sense-contents, which are themselves, as always, neither mental nor physical.

It is characteristic of some idealists, who are not Berkeleyans,

[1] Vide *The First Dialogue between Hylas and Philonous.*

to hold that "*x* is real," where *x* stands for a thing and not for a person, is equivalent to "*x* is thought of," so that it is self-contradictory to hold that anything exists unthought of, or that anything which is thought of is unreal. In support of the first of these consequences, it is argued that if I make any judgement whatsoever about a thing I must necessarily be thinking of it. But while it is true that the sentence "I judge that *x* exists" entails "*x* is thought of," it does not follow from this that it is self-contradictory to assert that anything unthought of exists. For the sentence "I judge that *x* exists" is plainly not equivalent to "*x* exists," nor does it entail it, nor is it entailed by it. I may very well judge that a thing exists which in fact does not exist, and a thing may very well exist without my judging that it does, or, indeed, without anybody's judging that it does, or without anybody's ever thinking of it. It is true that the fact that I assert that a thing exists shows that I am thinking of it, or have thought of it, but this does not mean that part of what I assert when I say that a thing exists is that I am thinking of it. It is essential here to distinguish between that of which the occurrence of a sentence is in fact evidence, and that which the sentence formally entails. Having made this distinction we can see that there is no formal contradiction involved in asserting that things which are un-thought of exist.

The view that whatever is thought of must necessarily be real is not confined to idealists. It depends, as Moore has shown,[1] upon the mistaken assumption that such a sentence as "Unicorns are thought of" is of the same logical form as "Lions are killed." "Lions are killed" does indeed entail "lions are real"; and so it is supposed that "unicorns are thought of" must analogously entail "unicorns are real." But, in fact, "being thought of" is not an attribute like "being killed," and there is, accordingly, no contradiction involved in asserting that such things as unicorns, or centaurs, although they are thought of, do not actually exist. The realist view that such imaginary objects "have real being," even though they do not exist, has already been shown to be metaphysical, and need not be further discussed.

It may be added that even if it were true that "*x* is real" was equivalent to "*x* is thought of," which we have shown not to be the case, the idealists' belief that everything that exists is mental

[1] *Philosophical Studies*, "The Conception of Reality."

would not thereby be justified. For "*x* is mental," is not entailed by "*x* is thought of," any more than by "*x* is perceived." Nor does this proposition that everything that exists is mental appear capable of being substantiated in any other way. For the fact that "*x* is real" does not formally entail "*x* is mental" proves that it is not an *a priori* truth. And while it is logically possible that all the things, such as houses and pens and books, which we believe to be unconscious are really conscious, it is highly improbable. For these things have never yet been observed to behave in the way which is characteristic of conscious beings. Chairs do not show any signs of purposive activity, nor do clothes appear to be sensitive to pain. And, in general, there is no empirical ground for supposing that what we ordinarily take to be material things are all conscious beings in disguise.

There remains still to be considered one empirical question which is a subject of controversy between realists and idealists. We have seen that the realists are justified in maintaining that it is not self-contradictory to assert that a thing exists unperceived; and we must now consider whether they have the right to maintain also that things do so exist in fact. Against them it has been argued that, even if things do in fact continue to exist when no one is perceiving them, we cannot have any good reason to suppose that they do.[1] For it is plainly impossible for anyone ever to observe a thing existing unobserved. But this argument is plausible only so long as the notion of unperceived existence is left unanalysed. As soon as we analyse it, we find that there can be a good inductive ground for believing that a thing exists unperceived. For what we are asserting when we say of a thing that it exists although no one is perceiving it is, as we have seen, that certain sense-contents would occur if certain conditions relating mainly to the faculties and position of an observer were fulfilled, but that in fact the conditions are not being fulfilled. And these are propositions which we do frequently have good reason to believe. For instance, the fact that I am now experiencing a series of sense-contents which belong to a table, a chair, and other material things, and that in similar circumstances I always have perceived these material things, and also remarked that other human beings perceived them, gives me a good inductive basis for the generalization that in such circumstances these material

[1] cf. W. Stace, "The Refutation of Realism," *Mind*, 1934.

things always are perceptible—a hypothesis whose validity is independent of the fact that at a given moment no one may actually be in a position to perceive them. Having now left my room, I have good reason to believe that these things are not in fact being perceived by anyone. For I observed that no one was there when I left, and I have observed that no one has since entered by the door or the window; and my past observations of the ways in which human beings make their entry into rooms gives me the right to assert that no one has entered the room in any other way. In addition, my past observations of the way in which material things come to be destroyed support my belief that if I were now in my room I should not be perceiving any such process of destruction. And thus, having shown that I may simultaneously have good reason to believe that no one is perceiving certain material things in my room, and also that if anyone were in my room he would be perceiving them, I have shown that it is possible to have good inductive grounds for believing that a material thing exists unperceived.

We have mentioned, also, that there may be good inductive grounds for believing in the existence of things which have never at any time been perceived. And this, too, can easily be shown with the help of an example. Suppose that flowers have been observed to grow at a certain altitude on all the mountains of a given range which have ever been climbed; and suppose that there is one mountain in the range which appears to be exactly like the others but happens never to have been climbed; in such a case we may infer by analogy that if anyone were to climb this mountain he would perceive flowers growing there also. And this is to say that we are entitled to regard it as probable that flowers do exist there, although they are never in fact perceived.

MONISM AND PLURALISM

Having dealt with the various aspects of the realist-idealist controversy, we come finally to treat of the dispute between monists and pluralists. We have, indeed, already remarked that the assertion that Reality is One, which it is characteristic of a monist to make and a pluralist to controvert, is nonsensical, since no empirical situation could have any bearing on its truth. But this metaphysical assertion is apt to be the outcome of certain logical errors which it is desirable to examine. And this we shall now proceed to do.

The line of argument which most monists pursue is this: everything in the world, they say, is related to everything else in some way or other; a proposition which for them is a tautology since they regard otherness as being a relation. And, further, they hold that every relation is internal to its terms. A thing is what it is, they declare, because it has the properties which it has. That is, all its properties, including all its relational properties, are constitutive of its essential nature. If it is deprived of any one of its properties, then, they say, it ceases to be the same thing. And from these premises it is deduced that to state any fact about a thing involves stating every fact about it, and that this involves stating every fact about everything. And this is tantamount to saying that any true proposition can be deduced from any other, from which it follows that any two sentences which express true propositions are equivalent. And this leads monists, who are given to using the words "truth" and "reality" interchangeably, to make the metaphysical assertion that Reality is One.

It should be added that it is admitted even by monists that the sentences which people actually use to express propositions that they believe to be true are not all equivalent to one another. But they regard this fact, not as throwing any doubt on their conclusion that every true proposition can be deduced from every other, but as showing that none of the propositions which anyone ever believes are in fact true. They say, indeed, that, while it is impossible for human beings ever to express wholly true propositions, they can, and do, express propositions which have a varying degree of truth. But what precisely they mean by this, and how they reconcile it with their premises, I have never yet been able to understand.

Clearly, the crucial step in the monist's argument, which leads him to such paradoxical conclusions, is the assumption that all the properties of a thing, including all its relational properties, are constitutive of its nature. And this assumption has only to be stated clearly and unambiguously for its falsity to become apparent. In the form in which we have stated it so far, which is the form in which it is commonly stated, it is not, indeed, unambiguous. For to speak of the nature of a thing may simply be a way of referring to the behaviour which is characteristic of it—

as in the sentence "It is in the nature of a cat to catch mice." But it may also, as we have seen, be a way of referring to the definition of a thing—as in the sentence "It is in the nature of an *a priori* proposition to be independent of experience." So that the words "all the properties of a thing are constitutive of its nature" may legitimately be used to express either the proposition that all the properties of a thing are relevant to its behaviour, or else the proposition that all the properties of a thing are defining properties of it. And it is not easy to tell from the writings of monists which of these propositions they wish to maintain. Sometimes, indeed, they seem to uphold both, without drawing a very clear distinction between them. But it is plain that it must be the second that they employ in the argument which we are now considering, whether they are aware of it or not. For even if it were true, which it is not, that it was necessary to take all the properties of a thing into account in order to predict its behaviour, it would not follow that every façt about the thing was logically deducible from every other. Whereas this conclusion does follow from the proposition that all the properties of a thing belong to it by definition. For, in that case, to assert that the thing exists at all is implicitly to assert every façt about it. But we know that to ascribe to a thing a property which belongs to it by definition is to express an analytic proposition, a tautology. And thus the assumption that all the properties of a thing are constitutive of its nature leads, in this usage, to the absurd consequence that it is impossible, even in principle, to express a synthetic fact about anything. And I regard this as being sufficient to show that the assumption is false.

What makes this false assumption superficially plausible is the ambiguity of such sentences as "If this thing had not got the properties which it has, it would not be what it is." To assert this may be to assert merely that if a thing has a property, it cannot also lack it—that if, for example, my newspaper is on the table in front of me, it is not the case that it is not on the table. And this is an analytic proposition whose validity no one would dispute. But to allow this is not to allow that all the properties which a thing has are defining properties. To say that if my newspaper were not on the table in front of me it would not be what it is, is false if it is equivalent to saying that it is necessary for my newspaper to be on the table in the sense in which it is necessary for it to contain news. For whereas the proposition that my newspaper contains news is analytic, the proposition that it is on the table in front of me is synthetic. It is self-contradictory to assert that my newspaper does not contain news, but it is not self-contradictory to assert that my newspaper is not on the table in front of me, although it happens to be false. And it is only when "A has not p" is a self-contradictory proposition that p can be said to be a defining, or internal, property of A.

In discussing this question, we have employed the factual terminology in which it is commonly presented, but this has not prevented us from recognising that it is linguistic in character. For we have seen that to say that a property p is a defining property of a thing A is equivalent to saying that the sentence which is formed out of the symbol "A" as subject and the symbol "p" as predicate expresses an analytic proposition.[1] And it must be added that the use of factual terminology is particularly inadvisable in this instance, because a predicate which serves to express an analytic proposition when combined with one descriptive phrase may serve to express a synthetic proposition when combined with another descriptive phrase which nevertheless refers to the same object. Thus to have written *Hamlet* is an internal property of the author of *Hamlet*, but not of the author of *Macbeth*, nor yet of Shakespeare. For it is self-contradictory to say that the author of *Hamlet* did not write *Hamlet*, but it is not self-contradictory, although it is false, to say that the author of *Macbeth* did not write *Hamlet*, or that Shakespeare did not write *Hamlet*. If we use the current factual terminology and say that it was logically necessary for the author of *Hamlet* to have written *Hamlet*, but not for Shakespeare or the author of *Macbeth*, or that Shakespeare and the author of *Macbeth* could conceivably have existed without writing *Hamlet* but the author of *Hamlet* could not, or that Shakespeare and the author of *Macbeth* would still have been themselves if they had not written *Hamlet* but the author of *Hamlet* would not, we should appear in each case to be contradicting ourselves; for we allow that the author of *Hamlet* is the same person as Shakespeare and as the author of *Macbeth*. But when it is recognised that these are simply ways of saying

[1] The passage which follows, down to the end of the paragraph, was incorporated also in a paper on "Internal Relations" which was read at the 1935 joint session of Mind Association and Aristotelian Society. See the *Supplementary Proceedings of the Aristotelian Society, 1935.*

that "the author of *Hamlet* wrote *Hamlet*" is an analytic proposition, whereas "Shakespeare wrote *Hamlet*" and "the author of *Macbeth* wrote *Hamlet*" are synthetic, the appearance of self-contradiction is completely removed.

With this we conclude our examination of the logical errors which give rise to the metaphysical doctrine of monism. But we must still mention that it is characteristic of a monist to affirm, and of a pluralist to deny, not only that every fact is logically contained in every other, but also that every event is causally connected with every other. There are some, indeed, who would say that the latter proposition could be derived from the former, on the ground that causality was itself a logical relation. But this would be a mistake. For if causality were a logical relation, then the contradictory of every true proposition which asserted a causal connection would be self-contradictory. But it is allowed even by those who maintain that causality is a logical relation that propositions which assert the existence either of general or of particular causal connections are synthetic. In Hume's phraseology, they are propositions concerning matters of fact. And we have shown that the validity of such propositions cannot be established *a priori*, as Hume himself made clear. "It implies no contradiction," he says, "that the course of nature may change, and that an object, seemingly like those which we have experienced, may be attended with different or contrary effects. May I not clearly and distinctly conceive, that a body, falling from the clouds, and which in all other respects resembles snow, has yet the taste of salt or feeling of fire? Is there any more intelligible proposition than to affirm, that all the trees will flourish in December and January, and decay in May and June? Now whatever is intelligible, and can be distinctly conceived, implies no contradiction, and can never be proved false by any demonstrative argument or abstract reasoning *a priori*."[1] Here Hume is supporting our contention that it is only by experience that the validity of synthetic propositions can be determined. Propositions which cannot be denied without self-contradiction are analytic. And it is to the class of synthetic propositions that those which assert causal connection belong.

We may conclude from this that the monistic doctrine that every event is causally connected with every other is logically

[1] *An Enquiry Concerning Human Understanding*, section iv.

independent of the other monistic doctrine which we have examined—that every fact is logically contained in every other. We have, indeed, no *a priori* ground either for accepting or for rejecting the doctrine that every event is causally connected with every other, but there are good empirical grounds for rejecting it, inasmuch as it denies the possibility of natural science. For it is plain that in making any given prediction we are able to consider only a limited set of data; what we do not take into account, we assume that we are entitled to ignore as irrelevant. I assume, for example, that in order to determine whether it will rain tomorrow I need not take into account the present state of mind of the Emperor of Manchukuo. If we were not entitled to make such assumptions, there would be no likelihood of our predictions ever being successful, for we should always be ignoring the greater part of the relevant data. The fact that our predictions are very often successful gives us reason to believe that some at least of our judgements of irrelevance are correct, and so to reject the monistic doctrine which denies their legitimacy.

It is important for us to expose the errors which are commonly associated with monism, because there is a sense in which we ourselves desire to uphold the unity of science. For we maintain that it is a mistake to conceive of the various "special sciences" as portraying different "aspects of reality." We have shown that all empirical hypotheses refer ultimately to our sense-contents. They all function alike as "rules for the anticipation of future experience"; and it is very seldom the case that, in making a particular prediction, we are guided by the hypotheses of only one science. What chiefly prevents this unity from being recognized at present is the unnecessary multiplicity of current scientific terminologies.[1]

For our part we are concerned to emphasize not so much the unity of science as the unity of philosophy with science. With regard to the relationship of philosophy and the empirical sciences, we have remarked that philosophy does not in any way compete with the sciences. It does not make any speculative

[1] What is required to put an end to this is the fulfilment of Leibnitz's hope for a "*Characteristica Universalis.*" Cf. Otto Neurath, "Einheitswissenschaft und Psychologie," *Einheitswissenschaft*, Heft I, and "Einheit der Wissenschaft als Aufgabe," *Erkenntnis*, Band V, Heft I. Also Rudolf Carnap, "Die physikalische Sprache als Universalsprache der Wissenschaft," *Erkenntnis*, Vol. II, 1932, and English translation, *The Unity of Science*, and "Die Aufgabe der Wissenschaftslogik," *Einheitswissenschaft*, Heft III.

assertions which could conflict with the speculative assertions of science, nor does it profess to venture into fields which lie beyond the scope of scientific investigation. Only the metaphysician does that, and produces nonsense as a result. And we have also pointed out that it is impossible merely by philosophizing to determine the validity of a coherent system of scientific propositions. For the question whether such a system is valid is always a question of empirical fact; and, therefore, the propositions of philosophy, since they are purely linguistic propositions, can have no bearing upon it. Thus the philosopher is not, *qua* philosopher, in a position to assess the value of any scientific theory; his function is simply to elucidate the theory by defining the symbols which occur in it.

It might be thought that the philosophical elucidation of scientific theories was required only for the popularization of science, and could not be of much benefit to the scientists themselves. But this would be a mistake. One has only to consider the importance to contemporary physics of Einstein's definition of simultaneity, in order to realise how necessary it is for the experimental physicist to be furnished with clear and definitive analyses of the concepts which he employs. And the need for such analyses is even greater in the less advanced sciences. For example, the failure of psychologists at the present time to emancipate themselves from metaphysics, and to co-ordinate their enquiries, is principally due to the use of symbols such as "intelligence" or "empathy" or "subconscious self," which are not precisely defined. The theories of psycho-analysts are particularly full of metaphysical elements which a philosophical elucidation of their symbols would remove. It would be the philosopher's business to make clear what was the real empirical content of the propositions of psycho-analysts, and what was their logical relationship to the propositions of behaviourists or *Gestalt* psychologists, a relationship at present obscured by unanalysed differences of terminology. And it can hardly be disputed that such a work of clarification would be favourable, if not essential, to the progress of the science as a whole.

But if science may be said to be blind without philosophy, it is true also that philosophy is virtually empty without science. For while the analysis of our everyday language is useful as a means of preventing, or exposing, a certain amount of metaphysics, the problems which it presents are not of such difficulty or complexity as to make it probable that they will remain long unsolved. Indeed we have dealt with most of them in the course of this book, including the problem of perception, which is perhaps the most difficult problem of those which are not essentially connected with the language of science; a fact which explains why it has played so large a part in the history of modern philosophy. What confronts the philosopher who finds that our everyday language has been sufficiently analysed is the task of clarifying the concepts of contemporary science. But for him to be able to achieve this, it is essential that he should understand science. If he is incapable of understanding the propositions of any science, then he is unable to fulfil the philosopher's function in the advancement of our knowledge. For he is unable to define the symbols which, most of all, require to be made clear.

It is indeed misleading to draw a sharp distinction, as we have been doing, between philosophy and science. What we should rather do is to distinguish between the speculative and the logical aspects of science, and assert that philosophy must develop into the logic of science. That is to say, we distinguish between the activity of formulating hypotheses, and the activity of displaying the logical relationship of these hypotheses and defining the symbols which occur in them. It is of no importance whether we call one who is engaged in the latter activity a philosopher or a scientist. What we must recognise is that it is necessary for a philosopher to become a scientist, in this sense, if he is to make any substantial contribution towards the growth of human knowledge.

INDEX

ABSOLUTE, THE, 36
Absolutism in ethics, 106–7
Æsthetic criticism, function of, 113–14
Æsthetic judgements, not objectively
    valid, 113
Agnosticism, 116
Altruism, 113
Ambiguous symbols, defined, 62–3
Analogy, argument from, as applied
    to other minds, 20, 128–9
Analysis, as the function of phil-
    osophy, 22–6, 31, 32, 51
    involves no metaphysical prin-
        ciples, 56
    is concerned with linguistic usages,
        57
    its logical character, 70
    its utility, 61–2, 68, 70
    nor empirical presuppositions, 57
    provides definitions *in use*, 24, 60
Analytic propositions, 5, 16, 31
    defined, 78–9
    how they increase our knowledge,
        79–80
    Kant's definition of, 77–9
    liable to be mistaken for synthetic
        propositions, 96–7
    their lack of factual independence
        of experience, 78–9
    their power to surprise us, 85–7
Ants, 78–9
A priori propositions, 16–18
    as tautologies, 31, 41, 47, 77–87,
        114–15, 135
    cannot serve as "first principles," 47
Aristotelian logicians, 60
Aristotle, primarily an analyst, 56
Atoms, 49, 136

"BASIC" PROPOSITIONS, 10
Being, as a metaphysical term, 42–3
Bentham, J., 55
Berkeley, George, his empiricism, 31,
    53–4; carried further by Hume,
    126, 141
    his analysis of the notion of a
        material thing, 53–4, 139–41

his idealism, 138–42
his mentalism, 143
his theism, 53–4
Berlin, I., 12 *n.*, 32
Black, M., 83 *n.*
Bradley, F., 34, 36 *n.*
Braithwaite, R. B., 24 *n.*
Broad, C. D., 16 *n.*

CAPITALISM, 88
Carnap, R., 32, 44 *n.*, 58 *n.*, 59 *n.*,
    91 *n.*, 130 *n.*, 140 *n.*, 151 *n.*
    uses a language in the analysis of
        itself, 71
Casuistry, 112
Categorical imperatives, 113
Causation, defined, 55
    not a logical relation, 55, 150
Characteristica Universalis, Leibnitz's
    desire for, 151 *n.*
Cogito ergo sum, a Cartesian fallacy,
    46–7
Colour blindness, 132
Communication, possibility of, 131–3
Consciousness, 130
Conservatism in science, 99
Continuity, direct and indirect, de-
    fined, 65–6
Contradiction, principle of, 77–8

DEFINITION, *explicit* AND *in use*, 59–61
Depth, as a property of visual and
    tactual sense-fields, 66–7
Descartes, R., his method, 46–7
    his mentalism, 142–3
Descriptions, definite, Bertrand Rus-
    sell's theory of, 22–4, 60–2
Diagrams, their use in geometry, 83
Domitian, 143
Duncan-Jones, Austin, 21 *n.*, 25 *n.*,
    26 *n.*

ECONOMY, PRINCIPLE OF, in scientific
    method, 97
Egotism, 113

Intuition as a method of arriving at
beliefs, 33, 129, 136–7
not a criterion of knowledge, 106,
118–20, 137–8
not essential in geometry, 83
not the basis of Descartes' method,
46

JEHOVAH, 116
Juhos, B. von, 90 n.

KANT, I., and arithmetic, 84
his account of necessary truths, 129
his belief in God, 114
his condemnation of transcendent
metaphysics, 34
his definitions of analytic and synthetic judgements, 77–9
his transcendental æsthetic, 84
his theory of morals, 112–13
his view of geometry, 82
his view of scientific method, 137
on empiricism, 74
primarily an analyst, 56
sees that existence is not an attribute, 43
Keynes, J. M., 49 n.

LANGFORD, C. H., 71 n., 81 n.
Language, its connection with logic,
79–80, 84–7
misleads metaphysicians, 42–5
scientific and emotive use of, 44
the subject of philosophical analysis, 26, 57–81
Laws of Nature, definitions or
hypotheses, 46, 69, 94, 95–7
Laws of thought, Aristotelian, as
tautologies, 81
Lazerowitz, M., 5 n., 9 n.
Leibnitz, 151 n.
Lewis, C. I., 71 n., 81 n., 102 n.
Limited independent variety, Keynes'
principle of, does not justify induction, 49
Linguistic propositions disguised in
factual terminology, 58–9, 149
rules, 17
Locke, J., as an analyst, 52–3
his misconception of matter, 53,
126, 129–30
Logic comprehends philosophy, 57;
and possibly mathematics, 82

concerned with definitions and
their consequences, and not with
empirical matters of fact, 31, 57,
74–7, 81
its ability to surprise us, 85–7
its truths are analytic, 77
Logical constructions defined, 63,
123
not fictitious objects, 63–4
Logistic, 71

MACE, C. A., 44 n.
Mach, E., 122, 137
Malcolm, Norman, 17 n., 18 n.
Marxists, 88
Material things as logical construc-
tions out of sense-contents, 53,
58–9, 63–8, 140–1
may exist unperceived, 145–6
Mathematics consists, like logic, of
analytic propositions, 31, 74–7
its ability to surprise us, 85–7
reducible to logic?, 82
Matter and mind, 123–5, 142
May Queens, 80
Meaning, an ambiguous term, 68–9
and principle of verification, 5
the word used in a variety of senses,
15–16
Memory, 126, 127
Menger, K., 81 n.
Metaphysicians not necessarily mys-
tics, 44–5
their statements not verifiable, 14
Metaphysics defined, 41
distinguished from philosophy,
51–2, 56, 57, 71
examples of, 39–44, 47, 88, 115,
126, 129–30, 135, 138, 146–7
how it arises, 33, 42–4, 45
its æsthetic value, 44–5
not literally significant, 16, 31,
35–45
Mill, J. S., a follower of Hume, 55
his conception of a material thing,
141
on logic and mathematics, 73–5
Mind, activity of, 137–8
and matter, 123–5, 142
Monism and causation, 150–1
and pluralism, 40, 146–51
metaphysical doctrine of, 40, 146–7
the outcome of logical errors,
147–50

157

A CATALOGUE OF SELECTED DOVER BOOKS
IN ALL FIELDS OF INTEREST

WHAT IS SCIENCE?, *N. Campbell*

The role of experiment and measurement, the function of mathematics, the nature of scientific laws, the difference between laws and theories, the limitations of science, and many similarly provocative topics are treated clearly and without technicalities by an eminent scientist. "Still an excellent introduction to scientific philosophy," H. Margenau in *Physics Today*. "A first-rate primer . . . deserves a wide audience," *Scientific American*. 192pp. 5⅜ x 8.

60043-2 Paperbound $1.25

THE NATURE OF LIGHT AND COLOUR IN THE OPEN AIR, *M. Minnaert*

Why are shadows sometimes blue, sometimes green, or other colors depending on the light and surroundings? What causes mirages? Why do multiple suns and moons appear in the sky? Professor Minnaert explains these unusual phenomena and hundreds of others in simple, easy-to-understand terms based on optical laws and the properties of light and color. No mathematics is required but artists, scientists, students, and everyone fascinated by these "tricks" of nature will find thousands of useful and amazing pieces of information. Hundreds of observational experiments are suggested which require no special equipment. 200 illustrations; 42 photos. xvi + 362pp. 5⅜ x 8.

20196-1 Paperbound $2.00

THE STRANGE STORY OF THE QUANTUM, AN ACCOUNT FOR THE GENERAL READER OF THE GROWTH OF IDEAS UNDERLYING OUR PRESENT ATOMIC KNOWLEDGE, *B. Hoffmann*

Presents lucidly and expertly, with barest amount of mathematics, the problems and theories which led to modern quantum physics. Dr. Hoffmann begins with the closing years of the 19th century, when certain trifling discrepancies were noticed, and with illuminating analogies and examples takes you through the brilliant concepts of Planck, Einstein, Pauli, Broglie, Bohr, Schroedinger, Heisenberg, Dirac, Sommerfeld, Feynman, etc. This edition includes a new, long postscript carrying the story through 1958. "Of the books attempting an account of the history and contents of our modern atomic physics which have come to my attention, this is the best," H. Margenau, Yale University, in *American Journal of Physics*. 32 tables and line illustrations. Index. 275pp. 5⅜ x 8.

20518-5 Paperbound $2.00

GREAT IDEAS OF MODERN MATHEMATICS: THEIR NATURE AND USE, *Jagjit Singh*

Reader with only high school math will understand main mathematical ideas of modern physics, astronomy, genetics, psychology, evolution, etc. better than many who use them as tools, but comprehend little of their basic structure. Author uses his wide knowledge of non-mathematical fields in brilliant exposition of differential equations, matrices, group theory, logic, statistics, problems of mathematical foundations, imaginary numbers, vectors, etc. Original publication. 2 appendixes. 2 indexes. 65 ills. 322pp. 5⅜ x 8.

20587-8 Paperbound $2.25

A CATALOGUE OF SELECTED DOVER BOOKS
IN ALL FIELDS OF INTEREST

THE MUSIC OF THE SPHERES: THE MATERIAL UNIVERSE—FROM ATOM
TO QUASAR, SIMPLY EXPLAINED, *Guy Murchie*
Vast compendium of fact, modern concept and theory, observed and calculated
data, historical background guides intelligent layman through the material
universe. Brilliant exposition of earth's construction, explanations for moon's
craters, atmospheric components of Venus and Mars (with data from recent
fly-by's), sun spots, sequences of star birth and death, neighboring galaxies,
contributions of Galileo, Tycho Brahe, Kepler, etc.; and (Vol. 2) construction
of the atom (describing newly discovered sigma and xi subatomic particles),
theories of sound, color and light, space and time, including relativity theory,
quantum theory, wave theory, probability theory, work of Newton, Maxwell,
Faraday, Einstein, de Broglie, etc. "Best presentation yet offered to the intelligent general reader," *Saturday Review*. Revised (1967). Index. 319 illustrations by the author. Total of xx + 644pp. 5⅜ x 8½.
21809-0, 21810-4 Two volume set, paperbound $5.00

FOUR LECTURES ON RELATIVITY AND SPACE, *Charles Proteus Steinmetz*
Lecture series, given by great mathematician and electrical engineer, generally
considered one of the best popular-level expositions of special and general
relativity theories and related questions. Steinmetz translates complex mathematical reasoning into language accessible to laymen through analogy, example
and comparison. Among topics covered are relativity of motion, location, time;
of mass; acceleration; 4-dimensional time-space; geometry of the gravitational
field; curvature and bending of space; non-Euclidean geometry. Index. 40
illustrations. x + 142pp. 5⅜ x 8½.   61771-8 Paperbound $1.35

HOW TO KNOW THE WILD FLOWERS, *Mrs. William Starr Dana*
Classic nature book that has introduced thousands to wonders of American
wild flowers. Color-season principle of organization is easy to use, even by
those with no botanical training, and the genial, refreshing discussions of
history, folklore, uses of over 1,000 native and escape flowers, foliage plants
are informative as well as fun to read. Over 170 full-page plates, collected from
several editions, may be colored in to make permanent records of finds. Revised
to conform with 1950 edition of Gray's Manual of Botany. xlii + 438pp.
5⅜ x 8½.   20332-8 Paperbound $2.50

MANUAL OF THE TREES OF NORTH AMERICA, *Charles Sprague Sargent*
Still unsurpassed as most comprehensive, reliable study of North American
tree characteristics, precise locations and distribution. By dean of American
dendrologists. Every tree native to U.S., Canada, Alaska; 185 genera, 717 species,
described in detail—leaves, flowers, fruit, winterbuds, bark, wood, growth
habits, etc. plus discussion of varieties and local variants, immaturity variations.
Over 100 keys, including unusual 11-page analytical key to genera, aid in
identification. 783 clear illustrations of flowers, fruit, leaves. An unmatched
permanent reference work for all nature lovers. Second enlarged (1926) edition.
Synopsis of families. Analytical key to genera. Glossary of technical terms.
Index. 783 illustrations, 1 map. Total of 982pp. 5⅜ x 8.
20277-1, 20278-X Two volume set, paperbound $6.00

IT'S FUN TO MAKE THINGS FROM SCRAP MATERIALS,
Evelyn Glantz Hershoff
What use are empty spools, tin cans, bottle tops? What can be made from rubber bands, clothes pins, paper clips, and buttons? This book provides simply worded instructions and large diagrams showing you how to make cookie cutters, toy trucks, paper turkeys, Halloween masks, telephone sets, aprons, linoleum block- and spatter prints — in all 399 projects! Many are easy enough for young children to figure out for themselves; some challenging enough to entertain adults; all are remarkably ingenious ways to make things from materials that cost pennies or less! Formerly "Scrap Fun for Everyone." Index. 214 illustrations. 373pp. 5⅜ x 8½.   21251-3 Paperbound $1.75

SYMBOLIC LOGIC and THE GAME OF LOGIC, *Lewis Carroll*
"Symbolic Logic" is not concerned with modern symbolic logic, but is instead a collection of over 380 problems posed with charm and imagination, using the syllogism and a fascinating diagrammatic method of drawing conclusions. In "The Game of Logic" Carroll's whimsical imagination devises a logical game played with 2 diagrams and counters (included) to manipulate hundreds of tricky syllogisms. The final section, "Hit or Miss" is a lagniappe of 101 additional puzzles in the delightful Carroll manner. Until this reprint edition, both of these books were rarities costing up to $15 each. Symbolic Logic: Index. xxxi + 199pp. The Game of Logic: 96pp. 2 vols. bound as one. 5⅜ x 8.
20492-8 Paperbound $2.50

MATHEMATICAL PUZZLES OF SAM LOYD, PART I
selected and edited by M. Gardner
Choice puzzles by the greatest American puzzle creator and innovator. Selected from his famous collection, "Cyclopedia of Puzzles," they retain the unique style and historical flavor of the originals. There are posers based on arithmetic, algebra, probability, game theory, route tracing, topology, counter and sliding block, operations research, geometrical dissection. Includes the famous "14-15" puzzle which was a national craze, and his "Horse of a Different Color" which sold millions of copies. 117 of his most ingenious puzzles in all. 120 line drawings and diagrams. Solutions. Selected references. xx + 167pp. 5⅜ x 8.
20498-7 Paperbound $1.35

STRING FIGURES AND HOW TO MAKE THEM, *Caroline Furness Jayne*
107 string figures plus variations selected from the best primitive and modern examples developed by Navajo, Apache, pygmies of Africa, Eskimo, in Europe, Australia, China, etc. The most readily understandable, easy-to-follow book in English on perennially popular recreation. Crystal-clear exposition; step-by-step diagrams. Everyone from kindergarten children to adults looking for unusual diversion will be endlessly amused. Index. Bibliography. Introduction by A. C. Haddon. 17 full-page plates, 960 illustrations. xxiii + 401pp. 5⅜ x 8½.
20152-X Paperbound $2.25

PAPER FOLDING FOR BEGINNERS, *W. D. Murray and F. J. Rigney*
A delightful introduction to the varied and entertaining Japanese art of origami (paper folding), with a full, crystal-clear text that anticipates every difficulty; over 275 clearly labeled diagrams of all important stages in creation. You get results at each stage, since complex figures are logically developed from simpler ones. 43 different pieces are explained: sailboats, frogs, roosters, etc. 6 photographic plates. 279 diagrams. 95pp. 5⅝ x 8⅜.
20713-7 Paperbound $1.00

PRINCIPLES OF ART HISTORY,
H. Wölfflin
Analyzing such terms as "baroque," "classic," "neoclassic," "primitive," "picturesque," and 164 different works by artists like Botticelli, van Cleve, Dürer, Hobbema, Holbein, Hals, Rembrandt, Titian, Brueghel, Vermeer, and many others, the author establishes the classifications of art history and style on a firm, concrete basis. This classic of art criticism shows what really occurred between the 14th-century primitives and the sophistication of the 18th century in terms of basic attitudes and philosophies. "A remarkable lesson in the art of seeing," *Sat. Rev. of Literature.* Translated from the 7th German edition. 150 illustrations. 254pp. 6⅛ x 9¼. 20276-3 Paperbound $2.25

PRIMITIVE ART,
Franz Boas
This authoritative and exhaustive work by a great American anthropologist covers the entire gamut of primitive art. Pottery, leatherwork, metal work, stone work, wood, basketry, are treated in detail. Theories of primitive art, historical depth in art history, technical virtuosity, unconscious levels of patterning, symbolism, styles, literature, music, dance, etc. A must book for the interested layman, the anthropologist, artist, handicrafter (hundreds of unusual motifs), and the historian. Over 900 illustrations (50 ceramic vessels, 12 totem poles, etc.). 376pp. 5⅜ x 8. 20025-6 Paperbound $2.50

THE GENTLEMAN AND CABINET MAKER'S DIRECTOR,
Thomas Chippendale
A reprint of the 1762 catalogue of furniture designs that went on to influence generations of English and Colonial and Early Republic American furniture makers. The 200 plates, most of them full-page sized, show Chippendale's designs for French (Louis XV), Gothic, and Chinese-manner chairs, sofas, canopy and dome beds, cornices, chamber organs, cabinets, shaving tables, commodes, picture frames, frets, candle stands, chimney pieces, decorations, etc. The drawings are all elegant and highly detailed; many include construction diagrams and elevations. A supplement of 24 photographs shows surviving pieces of original and Chippendale-style pieces of furniture. Brief biography of Chippendale by N. I. Bienenstock, editor of *Furniture World.* Reproduced from the 1762 edition. 200 plates, plus 19 photographic plates. vi + 249pp. 9⅛ x 12¼. 21601-2 Paperbound $3.50

AMERICAN ANTIQUE FURNITURE: A BOOK FOR AMATEURS,
Edgar G. Miller, Jr.
Standard introduction and practical guide to identification of valuable American antique furniture. 2115 illustrations, mostly photographs taken by the author in 148 private homes, are arranged in chronological order in extensive chapters on chairs, sofas, chests, desks, bedsteads, mirrors, tables, clocks, and other articles. Focus is on furniture accessible to the collector, including simpler pieces and a larger than usual coverage of Empire style. Introductory chapters identify structural elements, characteristics of various styles, how to avoid fakes, etc. "We are frequently asked to name some book on American furniture that will meet the requirements of the novice collector, the beginning dealer, and . . . the general public. . . . We believe Mr. Miller's two volumes more completely satisfy this specification than any other work," *Antiques.* Appendix. Index. Total of vi + 1106pp. 7⅞ x 10¾. 21599-7, 21600-4 Two volume set, paperbound $7.50

THE BAD CHILD'S BOOK OF BEASTS, MORE BEASTS FOR WORSE CHILDREN, and A MORAL ALPHABET, *H. Belloc*
Hardly and anthology of humorous verse has appeared in the last 50 years without at least a couple of these famous nonsense verses. But one must see the entire volumes — with all the delightful original illustrations by Sir Basil Blackwood — to appreciate fully Belloc's charming and witty verses that play so subacidly on the platitudes of life and morals that beset his day — and ours. A great humor classic. Three books in one. Total of 157pp. 5⅜ x 8.
20749-8 Paperbound $1.00

THE DEVIL'S DICTIONARY, *Ambrose Bierce*
Sardonic and irreverent barbs puncturing the pomposities and absurdities of American politics, business, religion, literature, and arts, by the country's greatest satirist in the classic tradition. Epigrammatic as Shaw, piercing as Swift, American as Mark Twain, Will Rogers, and Fred Allen, Bierce will always remain the favorite of a small coterie of enthusiasts, and of writers and speakers whom he supplies with "some of the most gorgeous witticisms of the English language" (H. L. Mencken). Over 1000 entries in alphabetical order. 144pp. 5⅜ x 8.
20487-1 Paperbound $1.00

THE COMPLETE NONSENSE OF EDWARD LEAR.
This is the only complete edition of this master of gentle madness available at a popular price. *A Book of Nonsense, Nonsense Songs, More Nonsense Songs and Stories* in their entirety with all the old favorites that have delighted children and adults for years. The Dong With A Luminous Nose, The Jumblies, The Owl and the Pussycat, and hundreds of other bits of wonderful nonsense. 214 limericks, 3 sets of Nonsense Botany, 5 Nonsense Alphabets, 546 drawings by Lear himself, and much more. 320pp. 5⅜ x 8. 20167-8 Paperbound $1.75

THE WIT AND HUMOR OF OSCAR WILDE, *ed. by Alvin Redman*
Wilde at his most brilliant, in 1000 epigrams exposing weaknesses and hypocrisies of "civilized" society. Divided into 49 categories—sin, wealth, women, America, etc.—to aid writers, speakers. Includes excerpts from his trials, books, plays, criticism. Formerly "The Epigrams of Oscar Wilde." Introduction by Vyvyan Holland, Wilde's only living son. Introductory essay by editor. 260pp. 5⅜ x 8.
20602-5 Paperbound $1.50

A CHILD'S PRIMER OF NATURAL HISTORY, *Oliver Herford*
Scarcely an anthology of whimsy and humor has appeared in the last 50 years without a contribution from Oliver Herford. Yet the works from which these examples are drawn have been almost impossible to obtain! Here at last are Herford's improbable definitions of a menagerie of familiar and weird animals, each verse illustrated by the author's own drawings. 24 drawings in 2 colors; 24 additional drawings. vii + 95pp. 6½ x 6. 21647-0 Paperbound $1.00

THE BROWNIES: THEIR BOOK, *Palmer Cox*
The book that made the Brownies a household word. Generations of readers have enjoyed the antics, predicaments and adventures of these jovial sprites, who emerge from the forest at night to play or to come to the aid of a deserving human. Delightful illustrations by the author decorate nearly every page. 24 short verse tales with 266 illustrations. 155pp. 6⅝ x 9¼.
21265-3 Paperbound $1.50

THE PRINCIPLES OF PSYCHOLOGY,
William James
The full long-course, unabridged, of one of the great classics of Western literature and science. Wonderfully lucid descriptions of human mental activity, the stream of thought, consciousness, time perception, memory, imagination, emotions, reason, abnormal phenomena, and similar topics. Original contributions are integrated with the work of such men as Berkeley, Binet, Mills, Darwin, Hume, Kant, Royce, Schopenhauer, Spinoza, Locke, Descartes, Galton, Wundt, Lotze, Herbart, Fechner, and scores of others. All contrasting interpretations of mental phenomena are examined in detail—introspective analysis, philosophical interpretation, and experimental research. "A classic," *Journal of Consulting Psychology.* "The main lines are as valid as ever," *Psychoanalytical Quarterly.* "Standard reading . . . a classic of interpretation," *Psychiatric Quarterly.* 94 illustrations. 1408pp. 5⅜ x 8.

20381-6, 20382-4 Two volume set, paperbound $6.00

VISUAL ILLUSIONS: THEIR CAUSES, CHARACTERISTICS AND APPLICATIONS,
M. Luckiesh
"Seeing is deceiving," asserts the author of this introduction to virtually every type of optical illusion known. The text both describes and explains the principles involved in color illusions, figure-ground, distance illusions, etc. 100 photographs, drawings and diagrams prove how easy it is to fool the sense: circles that aren't round, parallel lines that seem to bend, stationary figures that seem to move as you stare at them — illustration after illustration strains our credulity at what we see. Fascinating book from many points of view, from applications for artists, in camouflage, etc. to the psychology of vision. New introduction by William Ittleson, Dept. of Psychology, Queens College. Index. Bibliography. xxi + 252pp. 5⅜ x 8½. 21530-X Paperbound $1.50

FADS AND FALLACIES IN THE NAME OF SCIENCE,
Martin Gardner
This is the standard account of various cults, quack systems, and delusions which have masqueraded as science: hollow earth fanatics. Reich and orgone sex energy, dianetics, Atlantis, multiple moons, Forteanism, flying saucers, medical fallacies like iridiagnosis, zone therapy, etc. A new chapter has been added on Bridey Murphy, psionics, and other recent manifestations in this field. This is a fair, reasoned appraisal of eccentric theory which provides excellent inoculation against cleverly masked nonsense. "Should be read by everyone, scientist and non-scientist alike," R. T. Birge, Prof. Emeritus of Physics, Univ. of California; Former President, American Physical Society. Index. x + 365pp. 5⅜ x 8. 20394-8 Paperbound $2.00

ILLUSIONS AND DELUSIONS OF THE SUPERNATURAL AND THE OCCULT,
D. H. Rawcliffe
Holds up to rational examination hundreds of persistent delusions including crystal gazing, automatic writing, table turning, mediumistic trances, mental healing, stigmata, lycanthropy, live burial, the Indian Rope Trick, spiritualism, dowsing, telepathy, clairvoyance, ghosts, ESP, etc. The author explains and exposes the mental and physical deceptions involved, making this not only an exposé of supernatural phenomena, but a valuable exposition of characteristic types of abnormal psychology. Originally titled "The Psychology of the Occult." 14 illustrations. Index. 551pp. 5⅜ x 8. 20503-7 Paperbound $3.50

FAIRY TALE COLLECTIONS, *edited by Andrew Lang*
Andrew Lang's fairy tale collections make up the richest shelf-full of traditional children's stories anywhere available. Lang supervised the translation of stories from all over the world—familiar European tales collected by Grimm, animal stories from Negro Africa, myths of primitive Australia, stories from Russia, Hungary, Iceland, Japan, and many other countries. Lang's selection of translations are unusually high; many authorities consider that the most familiar tales find their best versions in these volumes. All collections are richly decorated and illustrated by H. J. Ford and other artists.

THE BLUE FAIRY BOOK. 37 stories. 138 illustrations. ix + 390pp. 5⅜ x 8½.
21437-0 Paperbound $1.95

THE GREEN FAIRY BOOK. 42 stories. 100 illustrations. xiii + 366pp. 5⅜ x 8½.
21439-7 Paperbound $1.75

THE BROWN FAIRY BOOK. 32 stories. 50 illustrations, 8 in color. xii + 350pp. 5⅜ x 8½.
21438-9 Paperbound $1.95

THE BEST TALES OF HOFFMANN, *edited by E. F. Bleiler*
10 stories by E. T. A. Hoffmann, one of the greatest of all writers of fantasy. The tales include "The Golden Flower Pot," "Automata," "A New Year's Eve Adventure," "Nutcracker and the King of Mice," "Sand-Man," and others. Vigorous characterizations of highly eccentric personalities, remarkably imaginative situations, and intensely fast pacing has made these tales popular all over the world for 150 years. Editor's introduction. 7 drawings by Hoffmann. xxxiii + 419pp. 5⅜ x 8½.
21793-0 Paperbound $2.25

GHOST AND HORROR STORIES OF AMBROSE BIERCE,
edited by E. F. Bleiler
Morbid, eerie, horrifying tales of possessed poets, shabby aristocrats, revived corpses, and haunted malefactors. Widely acknowledged as the best of their kind between Poe and the moderns, reflecting their author's inner torment and bitter view of life. Includes "Damned Thing," "The Middle Toe of the Right Foot," "The Eyes of the Panther," "Visions of the Night," "Moxon's Master," and over a dozen others. Editor's introduction. xxii + 199pp. 5⅜ x 8½.
20767-6 Paperbound $1.50

THREE GOTHIC NOVELS, *edited by E. F. Bleiler*
Originators of the still popular Gothic novel form, influential in ushering in early 19th-century Romanticism. Horace Walpole's *Castle of Otranto*, William Beckford's *Vathek*, John Polidori's *The Vampyre*, and a *Fragment* by Lord Byron are enjoyable as exciting reading or as documents in the history of English literature. Editor's introduction. xi + 291pp. 5⅜ x 8½.
21232-7 Paperbound $2.00

BEST GHOST STORIES OF LEFANU, *edited by E. F. Bleiler*
Though admired by such critics as V. S. Pritchett, Charles Dickens and Henry James, ghost stories by the Irish novelist Joseph Sheridan LeFanu have never become as widely known as his detective fiction. About half of the 16 stories in this collection have never before been available in America. Collection includes "Carmilla" (perhaps the best vampire story ever written), "The Haunted Baronet," "The Fortunes of Sir Robert Ardagh," and the classic "Green Tea." Editor's introduction. 7 contemporary illustrations. Portrait of LeFanu. xii + 467pp. 5⅜ x 8.
20415-4 Paperbound $2.50

EASY-TO-DO ENTERTAINMENTS AND DIVERSIONS WITH COINS, CARDS, STRING, PAPER AND MATCHES, *R. M. Abraham*
Over 300 tricks, games and puzzles will provide young readers with absorbing fun. Sections on card games; paper-folding; tricks with coins, matches and pieces of string; games for the agile; toy-making from common household objects; mathematical recreations; and 50 miscellaneous pastimes. Anyone in charge of groups of youngsters, including hard-pressed parents, and in need of suggestions on how to keep children sensibly amused and quietly content will find this book indispensable. Clear, simple text, copious number of delightful line drawings and illustrative diagrams. Originally titled "Winter Nights' Entertainments." Introduction by Lord Baden Powell. 329 illustrations. v + 186pp. 5⅜ x 8½.   20921-0 Paperbound $1.00

AN INTRODUCTION TO CHESS MOVES AND TACTICS SIMPLY EXPLAINED, *Leonard Barden*
Beginner's introduction to the royal game. Names, possible moves of the pieces, definitions of essential terms, how games are won, etc. explained in 30-odd pages. With this background you'll be able to sit right down and play. Balance of book teaches strategy — openings, middle game, typical endgame play, and suggestions for improving your game. A sample game is fully analyzed. True middle-level introduction, teaching you all the essentials without oversimplifying or losing you in a maze of detail. 58 figures. 102pp. 5⅜ x 8½.   21210-6 Paperbound $1.25

LASKER'S MANUAL OF CHESS, *Dr. Emanuel Lasker*
Probably the greatest chess player of modern times, Dr. Emanuel Lasker held the world championship 28 years, independent of passing schools or fashions. This unmatched study of the game, chiefly for intermediate to skilled players, analyzes basic methods, combinations, position play, the aesthetics of chess, dozens of different openings, etc., with constant reference to great modern games. Contains a brilliant exposition of Steinitz's important theories. Introduction by Fred Reinfeld. Tables of Lasker's tournament record. 3 indices. 308 diagrams. 1 photograph. xxx + 349pp. 5⅜ x 8.20640-8 Paperbound $2.50

COMBINATIONS: THE HEART OF CHESS, *Irving Chernev*
Step-by-step from simple combinations to complex, this book, by a well-known chess writer, shows you the intricacies of pins, counter-pins, knight forks, and smothered mates. Other chapters show alternate lines of play to those taken in actual championship games; boomerang combinations; classic examples of brilliant combination play by Nimzovich, Rubinstein, Tarrasch, Botvinnik, Alekhine and Capablanca. Index. 356 diagrams. ix + 245pp. 5⅜ x 8½.   21744-2 Paperbound $2.00

HOW TO SOLVE CHESS PROBLEMS, *K. S. Howard*
Full of practical suggestions for the fan or the beginner — who knows only the moves of the chessmen. Contains preliminary section and 58 two-move, 46 three-move, and 8 four-move problems composed by 27 outstanding American problem creators in the last 30 years. Explanation of all terms and exhaustive index. "Just what is wanted for the student," Brian Harley. 112 problems, solutions. vi + 171pp. 5⅜ x 8.   20748-X Paperbound $1.50

SOCIAL THOUGHT FROM LORE TO SCIENCE,
H. E. Barnes and H. Becker
An immense survey of sociological thought and ways of viewing, studying, planning, and reforming society from earliest times to the present. Includes thought on society of preliterate peoples, ancient non-Western cultures, and every great movement in Europe, America, and modern Japan. Analyzes hundreds of great thinkers: Plato, Augustine, Bodin, Vico, Montesquieu, Herder, Comte, Marx, etc. Weighs the contributions of utopians, sophists, fascists and communists; economists, jurists, philosophers, ecclesiastics, and every 19th and 20th century school of scientific sociology, anthropology, and social psychology throughout the world. Combines topical, chronological, and regional approaches, treating the evolution of social thought as a process rather than as a series of mere topics. "Impressive accuracy, competence, and discrimination . . . easily the best single survey," *Nation.* Thoroughly revised, with new material up to 1960. 2 indexes. Over 2200 bibliographical notes. Three volume set. Total of 1586pp. 5⅜ x 8.

20901-6, 20902-4, 20903-2 Three volume set, paperbound $9.00

A HISTORY OF HISTORICAL WRITING, *Harry Elmer Barnes*
Virtually the only adequate survey of the whole course of historical writing in a single volume. Surveys developments from the beginnings of historiography in the ancient Near East and the Classical World, up through the Cold War. Covers major historians in detail, shows interrelationship with cultural background, makes clear individual contributions, evaluates and estimates importance; also enormously rich upon minor authors and thinkers who are usually passed over. Packed with scholarship and learning, clear, easily written. Indispensable to every student of history. Revised and enlarged up to 1961. Index and bibliography. xv + 442pp. 5⅜ x 8½.

20104-X Paperbound $2.75

JOHANN SEBASTIAN BACH, *Philipp Spitta*
The complete and unabridged text of the definitive study of Bach. Written some 70 years ago, it is still unsurpassed for its coverage of nearly all aspects of Bach's life and work. There could hardly be a finer non-technical introduction to Bach's music than the detailed, lucid analyses which Spitta provides for hundreds of individual pieces. 26 solid pages are devoted to the B minor mass, for example, and 30 pages to the glorious St. Matthew Passion. This monumental set also includes a major analysis of the music of the 18th century: Buxtehude, Pachelbel, etc. "Unchallenged as the last word on one of the supreme geniuses of music," John Barkham, *Saturday Review Syndicate.* Total of 1819pp. Heavy cloth binding. 5⅜ x 8.

22278-0, 22279-9 Two volume set, clothbound $15.00

BEETHOVEN AND HIS NINE SYMPHONIES, *George Grove*
In this modern middle-level classic of musicology Grove not only analyzes all nine of Beethoven's symphonies very thoroughly in terms of their musical structure, but also discusses the circumstances under which they were written, Beethoven's stylistic development, and much other background material. This is an extremely rich book, yet very easily followed; it is highly recommended to anyone seriously interested in music. Over 250 musical passages. Index. viii + 407pp. 5⅜ x 8.

20334-4 Paperbound $2.25

THREE SCIENCE FICTION NOVELS,
John Taine
Acknowledged by many as the best SF writer of the 1920's, Taine (under the name Eric Temple Bell) was also a Professor of Mathematics of considerable renown. Reprinted here are *The Time Stream*, generally considered Taine's best, *The Greatest Game*, a biological-fiction novel, and *The Purple Sapphire*, involving a supercivilization of the past. Taine's stories tie fantastic narratives to frameworks of original and logical scientific concepts. Speculation is often profound on such questions as the nature of time, concept of entropy, cyclical universes, etc. 4 contemporary illustrations. v + 532pp. 5⅜ x 8⅜.

21180-0 Paperbound $2.50

SEVEN SCIENCE FICTION NOVELS,
H. G. Wells
Full unabridged texts of 7 science-fiction novels of the master. Ranging from biology, physics, chemistry, astronomy, to sociology and other studies, Mr. Wells extrapolates whole worlds of strange and intriguing character. "One will have to go far to match this for entertainment, excitement, and sheer pleasure . . ."*New York Times*. Contents: The Time Machine, The Island of Dr. Moreau, The First Men in the Moon, The Invisible Man, The War of the Worlds, The Food of the Gods, In The Days of the Comet. 1015pp. 5⅜ x 8.

20264-X Clothbound $5.00

28 SCIENCE FICTION STORIES OF H. G. WELLS.
Two full, unabridged novels, *Men Like Gods* and *Star Begotten*, plus 26 short stories by the master science-fiction writer of all time! Stories of space, time, invention, exploration, futuristic adventure. Partial contents: *The Country of the Blind, In the Abyss, The Crystal Egg, The Man Who Could Work Miracles, A Story of Days to Come, The Empire of the Ants, The Magic Shop, The Valley of the Spiders, A Story of the Stone Age, Under the Knife, Sea Raiders*, etc. An indispensable collection for the library of anyone interested in science fiction adventure. 928pp. 5⅜ x 8.

20265-8 Clothbound $5.00

THREE MARTIAN NOVELS,
Edgar Rice Burroughs
Complete, unabridged reprinting, in one volume, of Thuvia, Maid of Mars; Chessmen of Mars; The Master Mind of Mars. Hours of science-fiction adventure by a modern master storyteller. Reset in large clear type for easy reading. 16 illustrations by J. Allen St. John. vi + 490pp. 5⅜ x 8½.

20039-6 Paperbound $2.50

AN INTELLECTUAL AND CULTURAL HISTORY OF THE WESTERN WORLD,
Harry Elmer Barnes
Monumental 3-volume survey of intellectual development of Europe from primitive cultures to the present day. Every significant product of human intellect traced through history: art, literature, mathematics, physical sciences, medicine, music, technology, social sciences, religions, jurisprudence, education, etc. Presentation is lucid and specific, analyzing in detail specific discoveries, theories, literary works, and so on. Revised (1965) by recognized scholars in specialized fields under the direction of Prof. Barnes. Revised bibliography. Indexes. 24 illustrations. Total of xxix + 1318pp.

21275-0, 21276-9, 21277-7 Three volume set, paperbound $8.25

HEAR ME TALKIN' TO YA, *edited by Nat Shapiro and Nat Hentoff*
In their own words, Louis Armstrong, King Oliver, Fletcher Henderson, Bunk Johnson, Bix Beiderbecke, Billy Holiday, Fats Waller, Jelly Roll Morton, Duke Ellington, and many others comment on the origins of jazz in New Orleans and its growth in Chicago's South Side, Kansas City's jam sessions, Depression Harlem, and the modernism of the West Coast schools. Taken from taped conversations, letters, magazine articles, other first-hand sources. Editors' introduction. xvi + 429pp. 5⅜ x 8½.   21726-4 Paperbound $2.00

THE JOURNAL OF HENRY D. THOREAU
A 25-year record by the great American observer and critic, as complete a record of a great man's inner life as is anywhere available. Thoreau's Journals served him as raw material for his formal pieces, as a place where he could develop his ideas, as an outlet for his interests in wild life and plants, in writing as an art, in classics of literature, Walt Whitman and other contemporaries, in politics, slavery, individual's relation to the State, etc. The Journals present a portrait of a remarkable man, and are an observant social history. Unabridged republication of 1906 edition, Bradford Torrey and Francis H. Allen, editors. Illustrations. Total of 1888pp. 8⅜ x 12¼.
20312-3, 20313-1 Two volume set, clothbound $30.00

A SHAKESPEARIAN GRAMMAR, *E. A. Abbott*
Basic reference to Shakespeare and his contemporaries, explaining through thousands of quotations from Shakespeare, Jonson, Beaumont and Fletcher, North's *Plutarch* and other sources the grammatical usage differing from the modern. First published in 1870 and written by a scholar who spent much of his life isolating principles of Elizabethan language, the book is unlikely ever to be superseded. Indexes. xxiv + 511pp. 5⅜ x 8½. 21582-2 Paperbound $3.00

FOLK-LORE OF SHAKESPEARE, *T. F. Thistelton Dyer*
Classic study, drawing from Shakespeare a large body of references to supernatural beliefs, terminology of falconry and hunting, games and sports, good luck charms, marriage customs, folk medicines, superstitions about plants, animals, birds, argot of the underworld, sexual slang of London, proverbs, drinking customs, weather lore, and much else. From full compilation comes a mirror of the 17th-century popular mind. Index. ix + 526pp. 5⅜ x 8½.
21614-4 Paperbound $2.75

THE NEW VARIORUM SHAKESPEARE, *edited by H. H. Furness*
By far the richest editions of the plays ever produced in any country or language. Each volume contains complete text (usually First Folio) of the play, all variants in Quarto and other Folio texts, editorial changes by every major editor to Furness's own time (1900), footnotes to obscure references or language, extensive quotes from literature of Shakespearian criticism, essays on plot sources (often reprinting sources in full), and much more.

HAMLET, *edited by H. H. Furness*
Total of xxvi + 905pp. 5⅜ x 8½.
21004-9, 21005-7 Two volume set, paperbound $5.25

TWELFTH NIGHT, *edited by H. H. Furness*
Index. xxii + 434pp. 5⅜ x 8½.   21189-4 Paperbound $2.75

LA BOHEME BY GIACOMO PUCCINI,
translated and introduced by Ellen H. Bleiler
Complete handbook for the operagoer, with everything needed for full enjoyment except the musical score itself. Complete Italian libretto, with new, modern English line-by-line translation—the only libretto printing all repeats; biography of Puccini; the librettists; background to the opera, Murger's La Boheme, etc.; circumstances of composition and performances; plot summary; and pictorial section of 73 illustrations showing Puccini, famous singers and performances, etc. Large clear type for easy reading. 124pp. 5⅜ x 8½.
20404-9 Paperbound $1.25

ANTONIO STRADIVARI: HIS LIFE AND WORK (1644-1737),
W. Henry Hill, Arthur F. Hill, and Alfred E. Hill
Still the only book that really delves into life and art of the incomparable Italian craftsman, maker of the finest musical instruments in the world today. The authors, expert violin-makers themselves, discuss Stradivari's ancestry, his construction and finishing techniques, distinguished characteristics of many of his instruments and their locations. Included, too, is story of introduction of his instruments into France, England, first revelation of their supreme merit, and information on his labels, number of instruments made, prices, mystery of ingredients of his varnish, tone of pre-1684 Stradivari violin and changes between 1684 and 1690. An extremely interesting, informative account for all music lovers, from craftsman to concert-goer. Republication of original (1902) edition. New introduction by Sydney Beck, Head of Rare Book and Manuscript Collections, Music Division, New York Public Library. Analytical index by Rembert Wurlitzer. Appendixes. 68 illustrations. 30 full-page plates. 4 in color. xxvi + 315pp. 5⅜ x 8½.
20425-1 Paperbound $2.25

MUSICAL AUTOGRAPHS FROM MONTEVERDI TO HINDEMITH,
Emanuel Winternitz
For beauty, for intrinsic interest, for perspective on the composer's personality, for subtleties of phrasing, shading, emphasis indicated in the autograph but suppressed in the printed score, the mss. of musical composition are fascinating documents which repay close study in many different ways. This 2-volume work reprints facsimiles of mss. by virtually every major composer, and many minor figures—196 examples in all. A full text points out what can be learned from mss., analyzes each sample. Index. Bibliography. 18 figures. 196 plates. Total of 170pp. of text. 7⅞ x 10¾.
21312-9, 21313-7 Two volume set, paperbound $5.00

J. S. BACH,
Albert Schweitzer
One of the few great full-length studies of Bach's life and work, and the study upon which Schweitzer's renown as a musicologist rests. On first appearance (1911), revolutionized Bach performance. The only writer on Bach to be musicologist, performing musician, and student of history, theology and philosophy, Schweitzer contributes particularly full sections on history of German Protestant church music, theories on motivic pictorial representations in vocal music, and practical suggestions for performance. Translated by Ernest Newman. Indexes. 5 illustrations. 650 musical examples. Total of xix + 928pp. 5⅜ x 8½.
21631-4, 21632-2 Two volume set, paperbound $4.50

THE METHODS OF ETHICS, *Henry Sidgwick*
Propounding no organized system of its own, study subjects every major methodological approach to ethics to rigorous, objective analysis. Study discusses and relates ethical thought of Plato, Aristotle, Bentham, Clarke, Butler, Hobbes, Hume, Mill, Spencer, Kant, and dozens of others. Sidgwick retains conclusions from each system which follow from ethical premises, rejecting the faulty. Considered by many in the field to be among the most important treatises on ethical philosophy. Appendix. Index. xlvii + 528pp. 5⅜ x 8½.
21608-X Paperbound $2.50

TEUTONIC MYTHOLOGY, *Jakob Grimm*
A milestone in Western culture; the work which established on a modern basis the study of history of religions and comparative religions. 4-volume work assembles and interprets everything available on religious and folkloristic beliefs of Germanic people (including Scandinavians, Anglo-Saxons, etc.). Assembling material from such sources as Tacitus, surviving Old Norse and Icelandic texts, archeological remains, folktales, surviving superstitions, comparative traditions, linguistic analysis, etc. Grimm explores pagan deities, heroes, folklore of nature, religious practices, and every other area of pagan German belief. To this day, the unrivaled, definitive, exhaustive study. Translated by J. S. Stallybrass from 4th (1883) German edition. Indexes. Total of lxxvii + 1887pp. 5⅜ x 8½.
21602-0, 21603-9, 21604-7, 21605-5 Four volume set, paperbound $11.00

THE I CHING, *translated by James Legge*
Called "The Book of Changes" in English, this is one of the Five Classics edited by Confucius, basic and central to Chinese thought. Explains perhaps the most complex system of divination known, founded on the theory that all things happening at any one time have characteristic features which can be isolated and related. Significant in Oriental studies, in history of religions and philosophy, and also to Jungian psychoanalysis and other areas of modern European thought. Index. Appendixes. 6 plates. xxi + 448pp. 5⅜ x 8½.
21062-6 Paperbound $2.75

HISTORY OF ANCIENT PHILOSOPHY, *W. Windelband*
One of the clearest, most accurate comprehensive surveys of Greek and Roman philosophy. Discusses ancient philosophy in general, intellectual life in Greece in the 7th and 6th centuries B.C., Thales, Anaximander, Anaximenes, Heraclitus, the Eleatics, Empedocles, Anaxagoras, Leucippus, the Pythagoreans, the Sophists, Socrates, Democritus (20 pages), Plato (50 pages), Aristotle (70 pages), the Peripatetics, Stoics, Epicureans, Sceptics, Neo-platonists, Christian Apologists, etc. 2nd German edition translated by H. E. Cushman. xv + 393pp. 5⅜ x 8.
20357-3 Paperbound $2.25

THE PALACE OF PLEASURE, *William Painter*
Elizabethan versions of Italian and French novels from *The Decameron*, Cinthio, Straparola, Queen Margaret of Navarre, and other continental sources — the very work that provided Shakespeare and dozens of his contemporaries with many of their plots and sub-plots and, therefore, justly considered one of the most influential books in all English literature. It is also a book that any reader will still enjoy. Total of cviii + 1,224pp.
21691-8, 21692-6, 21693-4 Three volume set, paperbound $6.75

THE WONDERFUL WIZARD OF OZ, *L. F. Baum*
All the original W. W. Denslow illustrations in full color—as much a part of
"The Wizard" as Tenniel's drawings are of "Alice in Wonderland." "The
Wizard" is still America's best-loved fairy tale, in which, as the author expresses
it, "The wonderment and joy are retained and the heartaches and nightmares
left out." Now today's young readers can enjoy every word and wonderful picture of the original book. New introduction by Martin Gardner. A Baum
bibliography. 23 full-page color plates. viii + 268pp. 5⅜ x 8.
20691-2 Paperbound $1.95

THE MARVELOUS LAND OF OZ, *L. F. Baum*
This is the equally enchanting sequel to the "Wizard," continuing the adventures of the Scarecrow and the Tin Woodman. The hero this time is a little
boy named Tip, and all the delightful Oz magic is still present. This is the
Oz book with the Animated Saw-Horse, the Woggle-Bug, and Jack Pumpkin-
head. All the original John R. Neill illustrations, 10 in full color. 287pp.
5⅜ x 8. 20692-0 Paperbound $1.75

ALICE'S ADVENTURES UNDER GROUND, *Lewis Carroll*
The original *Alice in Wonderland*, hand-lettered and illustrated by Carroll
himself, and originally presented as a Christmas gift to a child-friend. Adults
as well as children will enjoy this charming volume, reproduced faithfully
in this Dover edition. While the story is essentially the same, there are slight
changes, and Carroll's spritely drawings present an intriguing alternative to
the famous Tenniel illustrations. One of the most popular books in Dover's
catalogue. Introduction by Martin Gardner. 38 illustrations. 128pp. 5⅜ x 8½.
21482-6 Paperbound $1.00

THE NURSERY "ALICE," *Lewis Carroll*
While most of us consider *Alice in Wonderland* a story for children of all
ages, Carroll himself felt it was beyond younger children. He therefore provided this simplified version, illustrated with the famous Tenniel drawings
enlarged and colored in delicate tints, for children aged "from Nought to
Five." Dover's edition of this now rare classic is a faithful copy of the 1889
printing, including 20 illustrations by Tenniel, and front and back covers
reproduced in full color. Introduction by Martin Gardner. xxiii + 67pp.
6⅛ x 9¼. 21610-1 Paperbound $1.75

THE STORY OF KING ARTHUR AND HIS KNIGHTS, *Howard Pyle*
A fast-paced, exciting retelling of the best known Arthurian legends for young
readers by one of America's best story tellers and illustrators. The sword
Excalibur, wooing of Guinevere, Merlin and his downfall, adventures of Sir
Pellias and Gawaine, and others. The pen and ink illustrations are vividly
imagined and wonderfully drawn. 41 illustrations. xviii + 313pp. 6⅛ x 9¼.
21445-1 Paperbound $2.00

Prices subject to change without notice.

Available at your book dealer or write for free catalogue to Dept. Adsci,
Dover Publications, Inc., 180 Varick St., N.Y., N.Y. 10014. Dover publishes more
than 150 books each year on science, elementary and advanced mathematics,
biology, music, art, literary history, social sciences and other areas.